MILITARY

AIRCRAFT

MARKINGS

MILITARY
AIRCRAFT
MARKINGS

BARRY C. WHEELER

LONGMEADOW
PRESS

This 1992 edition is published by
Longmeadow Press
201 High Ridge Road
Stamford, CT 06904

ISBN 0 681 41461 8

p. 2 (above): Day fighter scheme on an inter-war RAF Siskin
p. 2 (below): US Navy F/A-18 Hornet over desert country
p. 3: McDonnell Douglas F-4 Phantom II of 38th Tactical Reconnaissance Squadron, USAF
Zweibrucken

Produced by Mandarin Offset

Printed and bound in Hong Kong

0 9 8 7 6 5 4 3 2 1

CONTENTS

COLORS OF WAR AND PEACE

Why are aircraft painted and given markings? Basically, to protect the airframe against corrosion, assist in concealment from an enemy and provide some form of national or unit identity. Markings were the first to appear, followed by camouflage, the latter being a derivation of the French *camoufler* – to disguise. Most of the color schemes have been the result of particular requirements such as for aircraft operating over certain types of terrain like the jungle or over the sea, or for special roles. Given today's modern, high-performance combat aircraft, it would perhaps be logical to think that there is no real need for camouflage. After all, missiles are fired at targets beyond visual range, and with long distance radars it is generally accepted that the day of the close-conflict dogfight is now past. That may be so, but at low level, under the radar, a fast moving aircraft will need all the protection it can get if it is to reach its target, deliver its weapons and escape undetected. An enemy on combat air patrol will be looking out for just such an intruder, and if he is painted in the wrong scheme, the 'Mk 1 eyeball' could more easily pick him out against the background, be it terrain or sky.

Markings as well as camouflage have changed over the last 70 years. Basic national insignia, to indicate ownership,

German night fighter
insignia, 1944

34th Pursuit Squadron
USAAC insignia, 1934

was first used in the early years of this century and continues to be applied, mainly to the wings, fuselage and tail. Some insignia remain almost unaltered in design since they were first adopted during the First World War, others have changed either to reflect a move to a new national political status, or the size has diminished to provide a less visible marking which will not compromise the camouflaged finish. In addition to the national insignia, aircraft often carry badges, both official and unofficial, and examples of these can be found throughout these pages. Equally important is the small lettered stencilling on an airframe. This usually relates to the type of fuel carried, maintenance instructions, safety warnings and, on combat aircraft, information on the armament carried.

It is perhaps easier to understand the subject of aircraft colors if the background

to their origin is outlined. The French and Germans introduced the first practical national markings; one meter diameter roundels of red, white, and blue had appeared on French military aircraft as early as 1912, and the black and white cross *patee* was adopted by the German Air Service from the first weeks of the war.

In October 1914 Field HQ in France directed that British aircraft were to have the Union Jack marking painted under the lower wings. This insignia might have survived if the Cross of St George in the flag had not appeared similar to the German cross at a distance.

The British finally decided that the concentric circle marking was by far the best form of insignia and, following agreement with the French, the roundel was adopted but with the colors reversed, red in the center, white and a blue outer ring. With blue next to the rudder post, these colors also formed the tail insignia. Despite changes of color shade and marking size over the years, Britain, France and Germany still retain the basic designs.

Camouflage came late in 1915, when the German Air Service introduced a two-color disruptive scheme of green and brown with light blue on the undersurfaces; mauve or purple replaced the brown later in the war. In 1916, the Royal Flying Corps adopted dark-painted top surfaces on its aircraft, the color varying from green to khaki, while a natural finish was retained for the undersurfaces.

After the war most countries adopted formal types of national marking and applied these in particular styles and locations to obtain some orderliness compared with the rather haphazard way it had been done previously. In the USA, bright colors were used extensively, usually to designate squadrons or formation leaders, while in the Royal Air Force most fighter aircraft had a silver finish with only the minimum of colors.

Colors and markings during the Second World War were of great variety and this diversity can be seen in these pages. Disruptive schemes of two or more colors were widely used by most combatants. For instance, the RAF selected brown and green as being the best combination for overland flying and on the ground camouflage, later changing to green and gray when over-water operations became part of most daylight missions.

German thoroughness had deduced that gray formed a useful neutral color and this was introduced early in the war to supplement greens and light blue. The cross *patee* of the 1914–18 war gave way to a straight-edged design and the swastika of the Nazi party was painted on the fins or rudders of all aircraft.

Germany's allies, Italy and Japan, both used distinctive markings to identify their nationality. The former had a prominent white cross applied to the tail and three black *fasces* in a circle on the wings. A white fuselage band was an added feature and units usually painted their squadron number and/or badge over this. Japan's blood red disk marking appeared on all Army and Navy aircraft and apart from outlining variations, this remained consistent throughout the war and continues in use today. Green was a dominant color on Japanese aircraft although towards the end of the war unpainted fighters were regularly used as the urgent need for replacement machines prevented the application of camouflage.

American camouflage centered around the use of green for the upper surfaces and gray underneath with the star insignia above the port and below the starboard wings and on the fuselage sides. Fighter and bomber units in Europe used a letter coding system for ease of identification, following closely that employed by the RAF. Unofficial personal markings were widely used. During the later years of the war, Allied supremacy in the air led to the abandonment of camouflage by the USAAF and the use of natural metal finishes. This resulted in reduced production man-hours per aircraft and slightly increased performance.

Against Japan, US Army Air Force aircraft followed similar color changes to those in other war theaters. However, US Navy fighters used blue as a basic camouflage for over-water operations, starting

Flying Tige

American Volunteer Group insignia, China, 1942

Hell's Angel insignia, AVG, China, 1942

French GB 2/91 Squadron, 1950s

French 'Stork' Squadron emblem, 1940

with quite light shades but ending in 1945 with a dark glossy sea blue overall.

Reflecting the post-war peace, aircraft once again adopted natural finishes, but this period was relatively short and the Cold War and Korea prompted a move back to darker disruptive color schemes.

Research played a major part in the present gray camouflage carried by RAF fighter aircraft. Prompted by a requirement for a color scheme that would be as effective against the sky as against the ground, a counter-shaded scheme was eventually devised and in 1979, an RAF Phantom was painted in the new colors. The idea was to give the aircraft as neutral an appearance as possible, given the deep shadows cast by the airframe in certain lighting conditions. The top surface of the Phantom's inner wing section was sprayed a darker shade of gray than on the outer sections with an even lighter shade on the undersurfaces. The scheme was subsequently applied to RAF Tornado and Hawk aircraft and has also been adopted by Dutch and Swedish fighters.

Bomber aircraft of the RFC and RAF in the First World War generally operated at night and were given a black undersurface to reduce visual detection, while retaining dark green over the top surfaces. This combination was also used in the 1939–45 War with the addition of brown above.

On the "other" side, the Germans had conducted a number of trials to determine the best colors and patterning for its warplanes and had concluded that a combination of greens would form the ideal camouflage. With schwarzgrun and dunkelgrun applied in a hard-edged "splinter" pattern over the top surfaces and a light blue or hellblau underneath, the Luftwaffe's bomber units considered themselves well colored for the conflict. However, this dark scheme showed itself to have severe limitations on daylight missions conducted at heights of more than just a few hundred feet! Switching to night operations, black was used to cover the light undersides and the white elements in the national markings.

Post-war bomber markings and colors changed slowly, reverting from wartime hues to the silver finish of the American-supplied B-29s. Anti-flash white was the color applied to the RAF's V-bombers (Valiant, Victor, and Vulcan) to protect them from the results of a nuclear explosion rather than for any reason of concealment on the ground. This finish, complete with its low-visibility markings, gave way in 1964 to a scheme in keeping with the switch from high-level to low-level bombing – dark green and medium sea gray over all top surfaces with white retained underneath. An exception was the black given to the undersurfaces of the Vulcans used on the Black Buck flights during the Falklands War of 1982. The V-bombers gave way to the Tornado and its present scheme of green and gray.

Having ended the war with fleets of silver bombers, the USAF retained natural metal finish for its force of new B-47s and B-52s in the 1950s and early 1960s. With the Vietnam war, tactical bombers acquired a three-tone camouflage after initial operations in light gray coloring and soon this finish was to be found on the top surfaces of most aircraft engaged in conventional bombing of Viet Cong targets in North Vietnam. For night operations, black was sprayed over the undersurfaces and tails of the aircraft and this finish was also applied to the new F-111 when it was first deployed to SE Asia in 1968. The national insignia was reduced in size during this period and eventually the three main colors that formed the marking were replaced by a simple dark gray outline. The other major marking defined at this time was a fin code. These were large two-letter signs applied to the fins of most types of USAF aircraft and indicated the unit and often the base to which the aircraft was allocated.

USAF trials in the 1980s, showed that the typical terrain reflectance value for the earth (ignoring desert and snow) is approximately 11 percent and this became the reflectance target value for a new paint scheme which blended the aircraft outline more effectively into the background. Research showed that the most effective scheme comprised two shades of dark gray and one of dark green. More specialized is the overall radar-absorbing black paint applied to the new Northrop B-2 and Lockheed F-117 'Stealth' aircraft.

The general outline of camouflage and markings over the years shows clearly that a wide diversity of colors has been applied to military aircraft. In addition to those briefly covered there are the blues and grays designed for use by maritime aircraft, the bright distinctive schemes used on experimental and special duty aircraft and of course, aerobatic team aircraft of most nations have highly visible coloring for their air display flying.

The following illustrations have been chosen to illustrate the wide variety of colors and markings that have been applied to warplanes over the years. The subject is large and it is certain that it will remain a source of continuing fascination.

AVRO 504

Bomber/reconnaissance/trainer; first appeared in 1913 and used initially in bombing and recce roles by the Royal Flying Corps and Royal Naval Air Service; later used with great success as a trainer due to its docile handling qualities; production exceeded 8600.

504K, ROYAL FLYING CORPS TRAINING UNIT, 1918
This aircraft has a khaki-green finish with clear-doped undersurfaces.

504R, ESTONIAN AIR FORCE, TALLIN, 1928
Only a small number of this variant, known as the Gosport, were built.

504N, OXFORD UNIVERSITY AIR SQUADRON, UPPER HEYFORD, UK, MID-1930s
This was widely used by RAF flying-training schools between the wars. It also saw service with the Cambridge University Air Squadron.

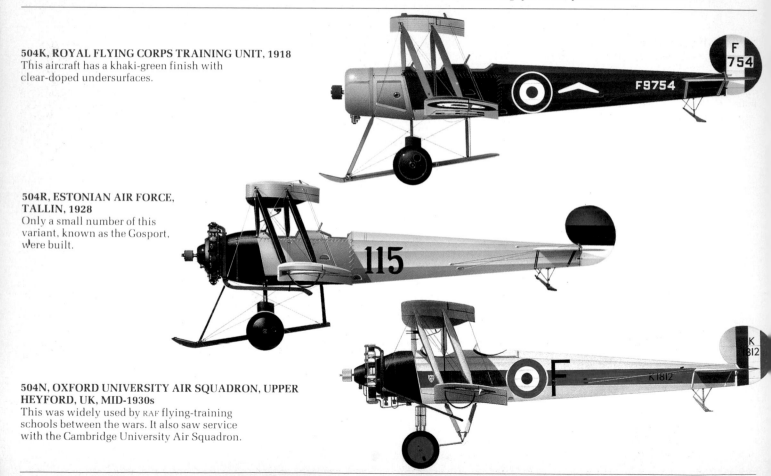

Fighter/reconnaissance; single-seater produced by the Royal Aircraft Factory at Farnborough; powered by a 200-hp Hispano-Suiza and later models by a 200-hp Wolseley Viper; single Vickers gun in fuselage and a Lewis gun above wing; 5205 manufactured.

74 SQUADRON, RAF, 1918
Major 'Mick' Mannock claimed some of his 73 victories flying this type shortly after the RAF was formed by the amalgamation of the RFC and the RNAS. Note the large identification letter 'A' on the fuselage. This 'A' code was also painted large on the upper starboard wing.

25th AERO SQUADRON, US AIR SERVICE, LANGLEY FIELD, US, 1919
This aircraft has retained the official PC10 or khaki top surface color, clear-doped undersides and rudder striping. Wartime roundels were officially replaced by the star insignia in May 1919.

SOPWITH CAMEL

Fighter; most famous World War 1 fighter renowned for its maneuverability; produced by Sopwith and others, notably Boulton & Paul; twin Vickers guns with Lewis gun above wing on naval version replacing one of the Vickers; 5490 manufactured.

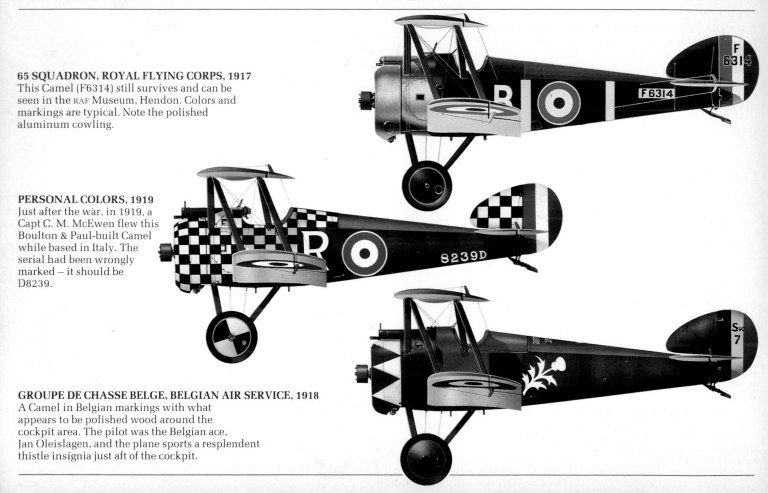

65 SQUADRON, ROYAL FLYING CORPS, 1917
This Camel (F6314) still survives and can be seen in the RAF Museum, Hendon. Colors and markings are typical. Note the polished aluminum cowling.

PERSONAL COLORS, 1919
Just after the war, in 1919, a Capt C. M. McEwen flew this Boulton & Paul-built Camel while based in Italy. The serial had been wrongly marked – it should be D8239.

GROUPE DE CHASSE BELGE, BELGIAN AIR SERVICE, 1918
A Camel in Belgian markings with what appears to be polished wood around the cockpit area. The pilot was the Belgian ace, Jan Oleislagen, and the plane sports a resplendent thistle insignia just aft of the cockpit.

Fighter; the plane was not a success as it had a structural weakness in the lower wing which marred an otherwise very streamlined design and resulted in a number of accidents; by the end of the war around 3000 had been built.

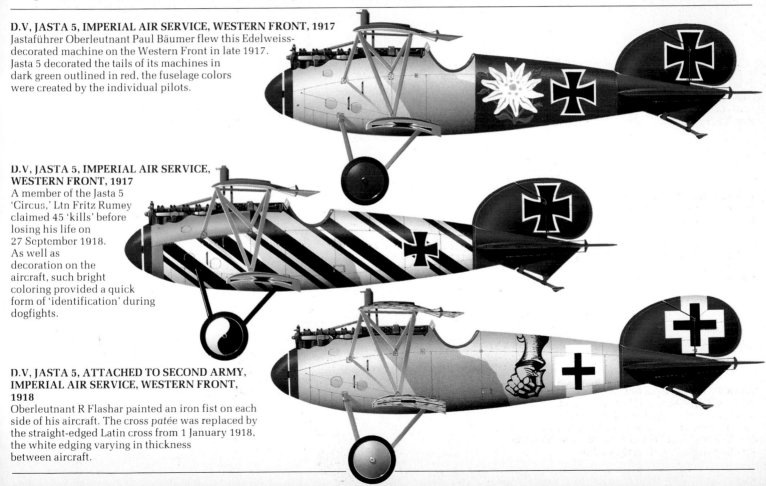

D.V, JASTA 5, IMPERIAL AIR SERVICE, WESTERN FRONT, 1917
Jastaführer Oberleutnant Paul Bäumer flew this Edelweiss-decorated machine on the Western Front in late 1917. Jasta 5 decorated the tails of its machines in dark green outlined in red, the fuselage colors were created by the individual pilots.

D.V, JASTA 5, IMPERIAL AIR SERVICE, WESTERN FRONT, 1917
A member of the Jasta 5 'Circus,' Ltn Fritz Rumey claimed 45 'kills' before losing his life on 27 September 1918. As well as decoration on the aircraft, such bright coloring provided a quick form of 'identification' during dogfights.

D.V, JASTA 5, ATTACHED TO SECOND ARMY, IMPERIAL AIR SERVICE, WESTERN FRONT, 1918
Oberleutnant R Flashar painted an iron fist on each side of his aircraft. The cross patée was replaced by the straight-edged Latin cross from 1 January 1918, the white edging varying in thickness between aircraft.

FOKKER Dr I

Fighter; 110-hp Oberursel rotary engine; two fixed 7.92mm MG guns with 1000 rounds of ammunition; about 320 manufactured; most famous German-built World War I plane, fast-climbing and highly maneuverable triplane; flown by the Red Baron, Manfred von Richthofen.

Dr I (213/17), JASTA BOELCKE, IMPERIAL AIR SERVICE, WESTERN FRONT, 1917
The aircraft of Ltn Fritz Kempf (whence the white letter K on the fuselage) finished in a dark olive green doped fabric, applied at the factory. Obscured by the lower strokes of the letter K is the Fokker serial (213/17) which was applied to all German aircraft, the number after the stroke being the year of manufacture.

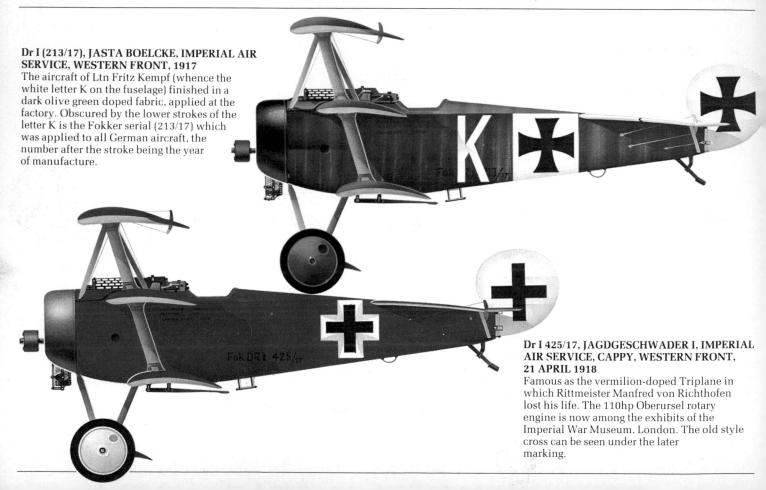

Dr I 425/17, JAGDGESCHWADER I, IMPERIAL AIR SERVICE, CAPPY, WESTERN FRONT, 21 APRIL 1918
Famous as the vermilion-doped Triplane in which Rittmeister Manfred von Richthofen lost his life. The 110hp Oberursel rotary engine is now among the exhibits of the Imperial War Museum, London. The old style cross can be seen under the later marking.

BRISTOL BULLDOG

Fighter; production models were the ii, iia, and iva and 441 were manufactured; almost half of these biplanes were exported to northern and eastern Europe; in mid-1930s, the Bristol Bulldog represented almost 70 per cent of Britain's airborne fighter force.

Mk IIA, 17 SQUADRON, RAF UPAVON, UK, 1934
The yellow represented on the spinner, wheels and rudder is the flight leader's color. Black zigzags seen on the fuselage were also applied over the silver-finished top wing surface.

Mk IVA, TLELV 35, FINNISH AIR FORCE, 1942
The yellow band and yellow wingtips were a standard identification feature. The Finnish Air Force bought 17 of this type in 1935 the last Bulldogs to be built.

Mk IIA (BRISTOL TYPE 105D), 1 ESKADRILLE, DANISH ARMY, 1932
This aircraft equipped Denmark's first fighter unit. The badge on the fin is a small 'Bulldog' insignia applied by the Bristol Company and is not a unit badge.

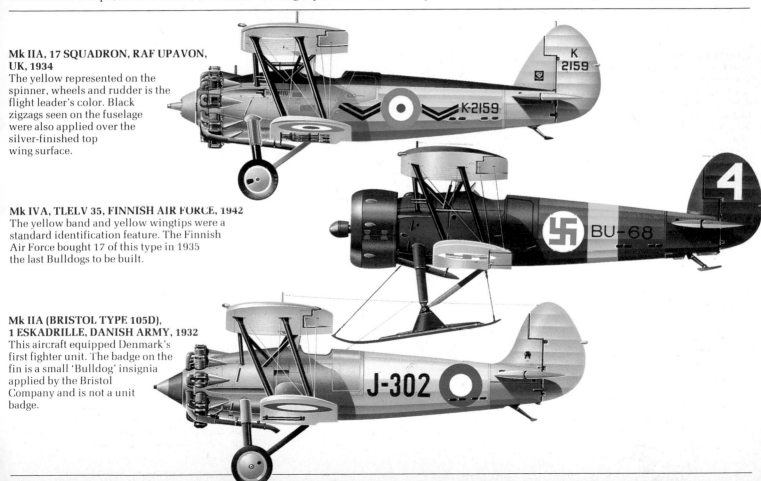

HAWKER HART

Light biplane bomber; bombload of 520lb underwing; single gun, .303 MG, in rear; 2700 manufactured, including similar aircraft developed from the Hart: Demon, Hector, Audax, Hardy and Osprey; the Hart could out-distance all fighters in service when first built.

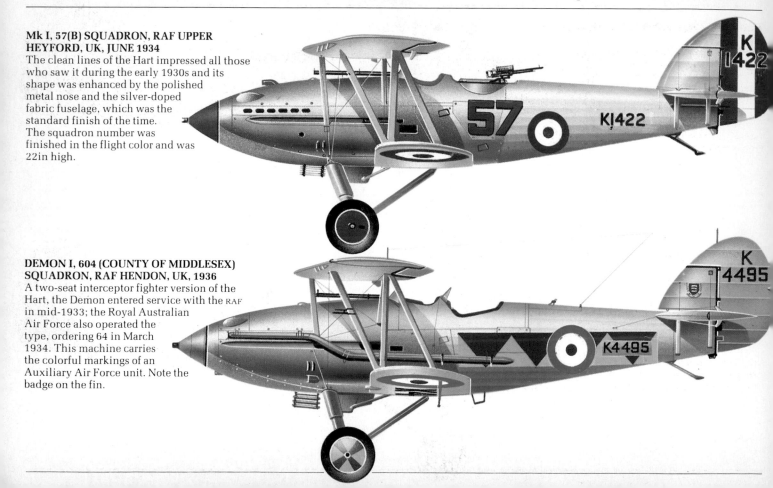

Mk I, 57(B) SQUADRON, RAF UPPER HEYFORD, UK, JUNE 1934
The clean lines of the Hart impressed all those who saw it during the early 1930s and its shape was enhanced by the polished metal nose and the silver-doped fabric fuselage, which was the standard finish of the time. The squadron number was finished in the flight color and was 22in high.

DEMON I, 604 (COUNTY OF MIDDLESEX) SQUADRON, RAF HENDON, UK, 1936
A two-seat interceptor fighter version of the Hart, the Demon entered service with the RAF in mid-1933; the Royal Australian Air Force also operated the type, ordering 64 in March 1934. This machine carries the colorful markings of an Auxiliary Air Force unit. Note the badge on the fin.

HAWKER FURY

Bomber/interceptor built by Hawker in UK and under license in Yugoslavia; prototype first flew in 1929; 264 manufactured, including 112 of more powerful Fury IIs.; originally named Hornet, the Fury was a fast and most elegant fighting biplane.

FURY I, 1(F) SQUADRON, RAF TANGMERE, UK, 1936–7
With their highly polished cowling and silver-doped fabric-covered airframe, the Furies came to epitomize the inter-war RAF fighter. As well as 1 Sqn, 25 and 43 also flew Fury Is, the latter unit being the first to equip. On the red fin is an arrowhead in white with a winged figure 1 in the center.

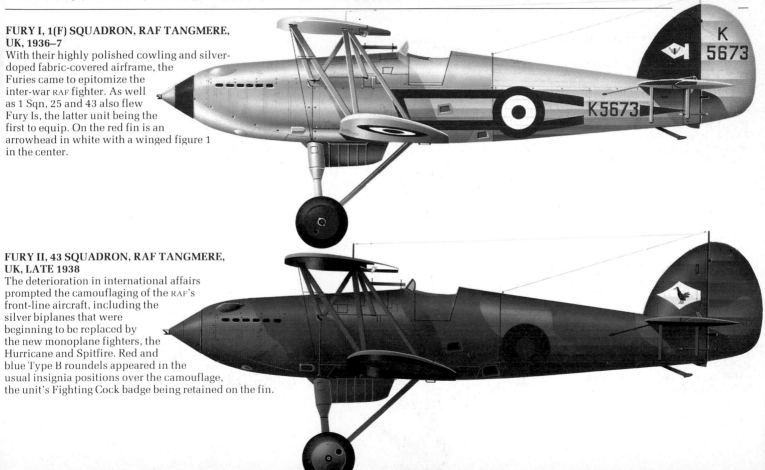

FURY II, 43 SQUADRON, RAF TANGMERE, UK, LATE 1938
The deterioration in international affairs prompted the camouflaging of the RAF's front-line aircraft, including the silver biplanes that were beginning to be replaced by the new monoplane fighters, the Hurricane and Spitfire. Red and blue Type B roundels appeared in the usual insignia positions over the camouflage, the unit's Fighting Cock badge being retained on the fin.

GRUMMAN G-5

Fighter; built for US Navy; prototype XFF 1 first flew in December 1931; Wright Cyclone engine in later models exceeded 200 mph; observers with strong arms were needed to operate the long jackscrew which retracted the main undercarriage after take off.

FF-1, VF-5B "RED RIPPERS," US NAVY, USS *LEXINGTON*, 1934–5
One of the 27 FF-1s ordered for use aboard Navy carriers and finished in the colors of the 3rd Section Leader of the Squadron. The blue tail denoted the *Lexington*, while under the cockpit is the boar's head unit insignia. From this ungainly looking Grumman design stemmed a range of aircraft that was to culminate in the Mach 2 Tomcat interceptor of today's Navy.

GOBLIN, 118 (F) SQUADRON, ROYAL CANADIAN AIR FORCE, DARTMOUTH, NOVA SCOTIA, CANADA, 1941
The Canadian machines were assembled by Canadian Car & Foundry, Grumman producing the fuselages and Brewster the wings and tail surfaces. Sixteen were taken on charge by the RCAF, this machine receiving the standard Dark Green and Dark Earth disruptive camouflage.

Plan view of No 344, RCAF, showing the upper surface pattern and positioning of the Type B wing roundels.

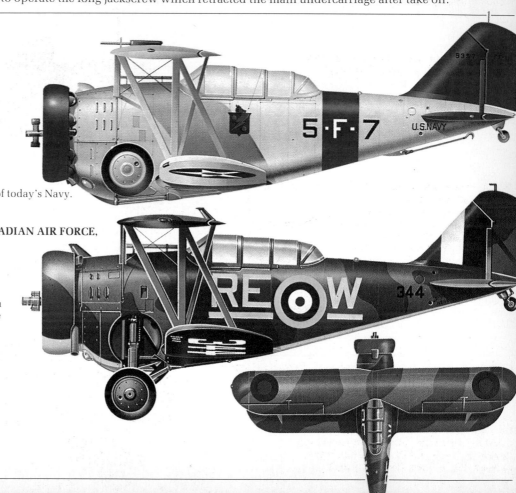

Fighter; all-metal monoplane nicknamed the 'Peashooter' by the USAAC; conservative features still held sway with an open cockpit, external wire bracing and a fixed undercarriage; 136 manufactured with many exported to Central America and the Far East.

P-26B, US ARMY AIR CORPS, JUNE 1934
One of two aircraft given the B sub-type designation, this machine has a fuel-injection system and also incorporated wing flaps, which the Army considered necessary owing to the P-26A's high landing speed.

P-26A, 95th PURSUIT SQUADRON, 17th ATTACK GROUP, USAAC, 1934
As with other aircraft at this time, the Olive Drab was replaced by Blue during the year. Standard armament of the P-26A comprised two .30in MGs, or one .30in and one .50in MG, with provision for light bombs under the fuselage and wings.

Bucking Mule marking of the 95th Pursuit Sqn.

P-26A, 34th PURSUIT SQUADRON, 17th PURSUIT GROUP, USAAC, MARCH FIELD, USA, 1935
An aircraft specially painted for a camouflage evaluation in a disruptive scheme of Desert Sand with random patches of Olive Drab and Gray over-sprayed. This was not adopted as a standard scheme, although variations on it were used in World War II, particularly in North African operations from 1942.

BRISTOL BLENHEIM 1

Fighter; the RAF's first all-metal stressed skin monoplane, it outshone most biplane fighters in the late 1930s but stood little chance against the German Bf 109 during the early daylight operations of WWII; in excess of 1450 of the Mark I manufactured.

Mk I, 114 SQUADRON, RAF WYTON, UK, SUMMER 1937
The first unit to be equipped with Blenheims, 114 Sqn received its original complement of 12 aircraft in March 1937. Camouflage was Dark Green, Dark Earth and matt Black, with the unit number applied on the rear fuselage. Code letters FD in gray replaced the unit number in 1938.

Mk IF, 54 OPERATIONAL TRAINING UNIT, RAF, SEPTEMBER 1941
It was as a night fighter that the early Blenheim proved successful. Some 200 were converted with an under-fuselage tray of four machine guns and AI (air-interception) radar. YX-N is finished in Special Night (Black) overall.

Mk I, ROMANIAN SQUADRON 1/3, EASTERN FRONT, AUGUST 1944
The survivors of 13 UK-built aircraft supplied in November 1939 were operating against the Russians in late 1944 as part of Luftwaffe Air Fleet 4 in the Black Sea area. Yellow fuselage band and wingtips denote the war theater, while 37 is probably the individual aircraft number.

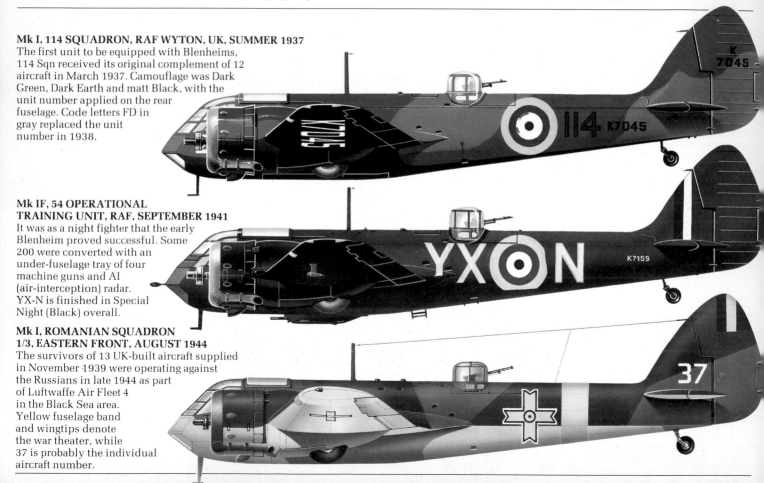

Fighter; the last of the open cockpit variety to see service with the RAF. Powered by a Bristol Mercury engine, it could reach 230 mph, making it the fastest fighter in RAF service between 1935 and 1937; production totaled 228.

Mk II, 151 SQUADRON, RAF NORTH WEALD, UK, 1937
Compared with the Mk I, this version has constructional changes to rationalize production methods, and some machines were fitted with a three-bladed propeller in place of the more usual two-bladed wooden type. All-over silver with unit markings on fuselage and across the top wing between the roundels.

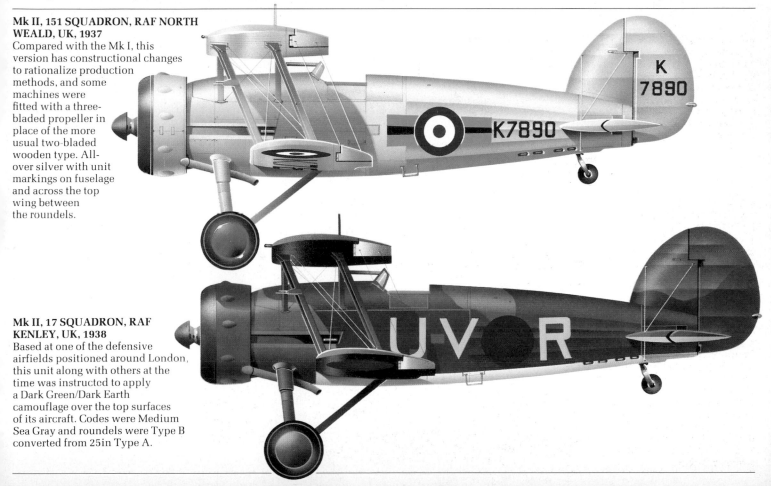

Mk II, 17 SQUADRON, RAF KENLEY, UK, 1938
Based at one of the defensive airfields positioned around London, this unit along with others at the time was instructed to apply a Dark Green/Dark Earth camouflage over the top surfaces of its aircraft. Codes were Medium Sea Gray and roundels were Type B converted from 25in Type A.

DOUGLAS DC-3

Transport; arguably the greatest airliner ever made, over 14,000 examples were manufactured in US, Japan and Soviet Union; also known as C-47, Dakota and Skytrain, the plane is still in service around the world more than 55 years after it first entered service.

DC-3, KLM (ROYAL DUTCH AIRLINES), SCHIPHOL, NETHERLANDS, SEPTEMBER 1939

Clearly marked with the country name on both sides of the fuselage roof, PH-ASK "Kemphaan" endeavored to ensure unviolated passage around northern Europe in the months before Holland fell to the Germans. It was eventually captured by the Luftwaffe in Norway.

C-47A-65-DL, FIRST AIR COMMANDO, USAAF, 10th AF, CHINA-BURMA-INDIA THEATER, 1944–5

Olive Drab and Neutral Gray was the scheme, but the finish was often worn from non-stop operations in a part of the world where air transport was vital to the Allies' war effort. This was one of 13 aircraft in the First Air Commando Force, and later received five diagonal white stripes around the rear fuselage.

DAKOTA III, 267 SQUADRON, RAF, ARAXOS, GREECE, 1944

An indeterminate scheme of browns with a light blue underside is the interpreted finish of FD857, alias C-47 c/n 9325. Of more than 1200 Dakotas supplied to the RAF under Lend-Lease, about 950 were of the Mk III version, 25 RAF squadrons flew Dakotas during the war.

Transport/bomber; entered military service in 1933; used by the German Condor Legion in Spain in 1937 and during World War II in all major theaters of operations by the Luftwaffe; a docile undemanding plane, over 5000 were maufactured.

Ju 52/3mg3e, KAMPFGRUPPE 88, LEGION CONDOR, SPAIN, LATE 1936
Three 12-aircraft Staffeln of Ju 52 bombers arrived in Spain toward the end of 1936 and operated alongside similar aircraft supplied to Franco by Germany in the summer. Color was a pale green-gray, probably Grau 63.

Ju 52/3MG4e, Stab IV/KGzbV 1, LUFTWAFFE, BALKANS, APRIL–MAY 1941
Wearing the yellow theater colors of the southern area of operations, this aircraft took part in the airborne invasion of Crete, called by Gen Kurt Student "the graveyard of the German paratrooper" owing to the high losses sustained. The letters KGzbV stand for Kampfgesch wader zur besonderen Verwendung (Battle Group for Special Duties).

Ju 52/3mg6e, IV/KGzbV 1, LUFTWAFFE, STALINGRAD FRONT, USSR, WINTER 1942-3
To reduce visibility against snow when flying supply missions to the beleagured 6th Army outside Stalingrad, aircraft were given a white water-soluble paint finish over the upper surfaces. A dark green surround has been left around the fuselage cross and swastika marking.

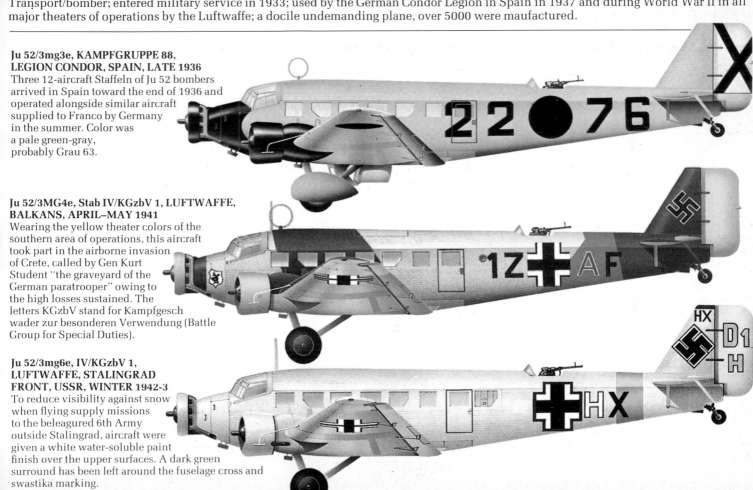

FAIREY SWORDFISH

Torpedo-bomber biplane; though outdated at the start of World War II the Swordfish remained in service with the Royal Navy as there was no replacement; its battle honours included the crippling of the Italian Fleet at Taranto and the torpedoing of the Bismarck.

Mk I, 823 SQUADRON, FLEET AIR ARM, HMS *GLORIOUS*, 1936

Developed initially from the TSR I (Torpedo-Spotter-Reconnaissance) and the modified TSR II which flew in April 1934, the Swordfish entered service in July 1936; by 1939 13 squadrons were equipped. Early aircraft were finished in silver overall with a color/number code on the fuselage side (yellow for *Glorious*, 804 call sign code number). Black fuselage decking and fin.

Mk I, 821 SQUADRON, FLEET AIR ARM, HMS *ARK ROYAL*, 1940

Early war markings on a carrier-based aircraft with Sky color undersides extending up to a line along the fuselage to meet the temperate gray/green pattern which was painted on the top surfaces. Eight inch serial and large figure/letter code indicate a carrier-based aircraft.

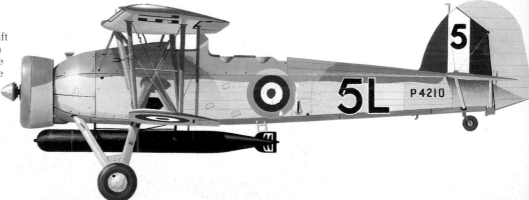

Medium bomber; one of the chief aircraft used during the Battle of Britain bomber offensive; more than 7300 manufactured. A slow, cumbersome plane, the He 111 needed fighter protection during daytime raids. Later used in night time operations.

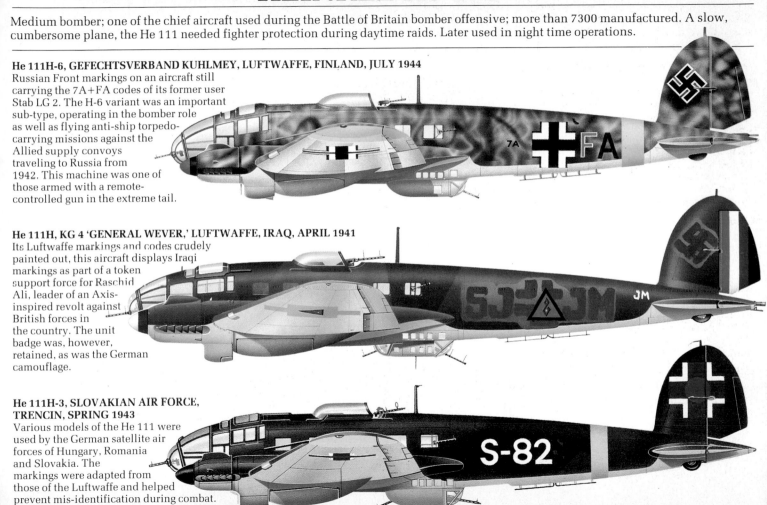

He 111H-6, GEFECHTSVERBAND KUHLMEY, LUFTWAFFE, FINLAND, JULY 1944
Russian Front markings on an aircraft still carrying the 7A+FA codes of its former user Stab LG 2. The H-6 variant was an important sub-type, operating in the bomber role as well as flying anti-ship torpedo-carrying missions against the Allied supply convoys traveling to Russia from 1942. This machine was one of those armed with a remote-controlled gun in the extreme tail.

He 111H, KG 4 'GENERAL WEVER,' LUFTWAFFE, IRAQ, APRIL 1941
Its Luftwaffe markings and codes crudely painted out, this aircraft displays Iraqi markings as part of a token support force for Raschid Ali, leader of an Axis-inspired revolt against British forces in the country. The unit badge was, however, retained, as was the German camouflage.

He 111H-3, SLOVAKIAN AIR FORCE, TRENCIN, SPRING 1943
Various models of the He 111 were used by the German satellite air forces of Hungary, Romania and Slovakia. The markings were adapted from those of the Luftwaffe and helped prevent mis-identification during combat.

SAVOIA-MARCHETTI S.M.79

Torpedo bomber/reconnaissance; one of the Regia Aeronautica's most successful aircraft, well liked by its crews for its ability to absorb considerable combat damage yet remain flying; prototype first flew in 1934 and was still being used by the Lebanese air force in 1956.

S.M.79/P.XI, 257 SQUADRIGLIA, 108 GRUPPO, REGIA AERONAUTICA, SICILY, 1941
The dorsal gunner's position gave rise to the sobriquet *Gobbo* (hunchback) for the aircraft. Color schemes varied; this dark painted machine carrying its almost indistinct unit number on the fuselage and a badge on the fin.

S.M.79/P.XI, 283 SQUADRIGLIA, 130 GRUPPO AUTONOMO, REGIA AERONAUTICA, MEDITERRANEAN, 1942
The Italian *Aerosiluranti* or torpedo-bombing units led the world in equipment and technique, a claim underlined by their success against Allied shipping. A white theater band circled the fuselage on this mottle camouflaged example.

S.M.79/P.XI, 193 SQUADRIGLIA, 87 GRUPPO, REGIA AERONAUTICA, SICILY, 1941
Dark Green with Yellow Ocher sprayed in random form was typical of the schemes applied to Italian Air Force aircraft of this period. On the center engine cowling is a single *fasces* marking; on the rudder cross is the badge of the House of Savoy.

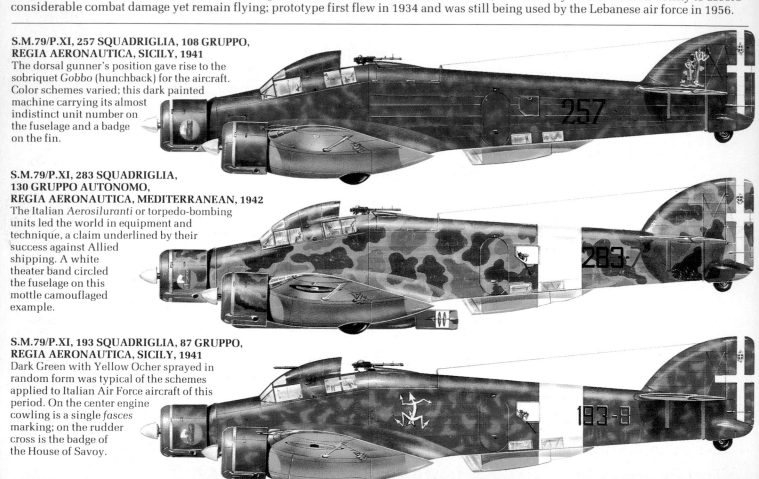

Dive-bomber; originally a monoplane with a parasol wing but re-designed into carrier-based dive-bomber/combat biplane for US Navy; delivered in 1937 it became obsolete even before World War II and was kept well away from the formidable Axis fighters.

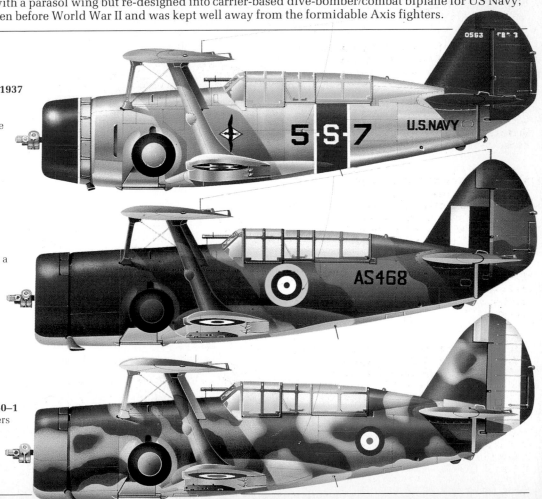

SBC-3, VS-5, US NAVY, USS *YORKTOWN*, 1937
These initial aircraft were delivered and operated in natural metal finish, apart from the chrome yellow on the upper wing surface and the red tail, the latter signifying the *Yorktown*. The blue areas denoted the 3rd section leader. Scouting Five's "Man O'War Bird" emblem is seen below the cockpit.

SBC-4 (CLEVELAND 1), RAF LITTLE RISSINGTON, UK, SEPTEMBER 1940
Five Helldivers found their way to the UK as a residue of 50 handed over to France by the USN. Sprayed Dark Green, Dark Earth with Sky undersides, the aircraft were used as ground instructional airframes.

SBC-4, AERONAVALE, MARTINIQUE, 1940–1
Fifty of these obsolete carrier biplane bombers had been ordered by the French Navy, most ending up on Martinique. Camouflage was Green and Gray with Sky Blue undersides.

GLOSTER GLADIATOR

Fighter; the Gladiator was the last of the RAF's biplane fighters and was withdrawn from frontline use by the end of 1941; it had fought with distinction in the Norwegian campaign and against the Regia Aeronautica in Malta, Greece and the Western Desert.

Mk I, F19, FINNISH AIR FORCE, KEMI, NORTH FINLAND, 1940
A ski-equipped J8 (Swedish designation) of the Swedish voluntary unit F19 during the Winter War against the USSR. Finland received 39 Mk IIs from the UK in 1940 and operated them until 1945. They were coded GL-251 to -280.

Mk II, 25 SQUADRON, RAF, UK, 1940
Early war camouflage of Dark Green and Dark Earth with Sky undersurfaces on an aircraft relegated to second-line duties. Unusually, the unit code ZK has no accompanying letter indicating the individual aircraft within the squadron.

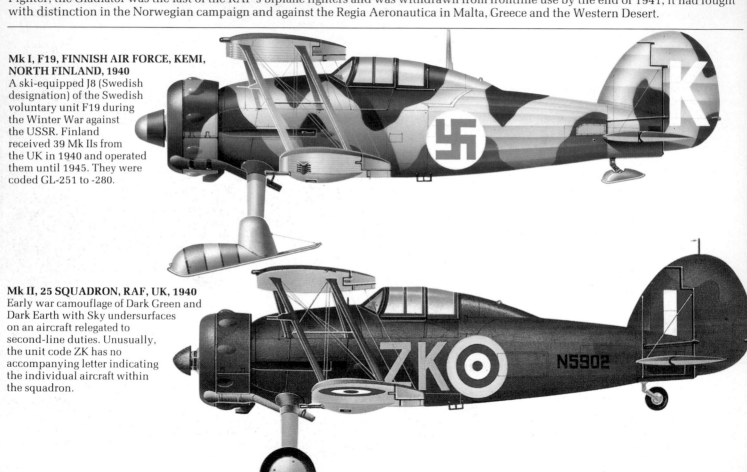

HAWKER HURRICANE

Single-seat fighter-bomber; carried bombs, rockets, tank-busting cannons and machine guns; 14,231 manufactured, including Canadian models; rugged and durable, the Hurricane was not as fast as the Messerschmitt Bf109, but could absorb considerable battle damage.

Mk I, 85 SQUADRON, RAF DEBDEN, UK, 1940
This has the Battle of Britain finish, with Sky undersides and the unit badge under the cockpit. Note the rudder flash size and position.

Mk IIC, 1 SQUADRON, RAF TANGMERE, UK, 1942
This has standard day-fighter colors, with Sky spinner and a yellow wing leading edge. The black serial has been applied over the rear identification band.

SEA HURRICANE (HURRICANE X), 440 SQUADRON, ROYAL CANADIAN AIR FORCE, 1942
Although built in Canada for the Royal Navy and finished in these colors, this aircraft was retained for use in Canada.

BOEING B-17

Bomber; known as the 'Flying Fortress', it bore the brunt of the USAF daylight bombing effort over Europe between 1942-45; first flown in July 1935, the earlier B17C was less than successful, but the aircraft's true worth was recognized with the later F and G series.

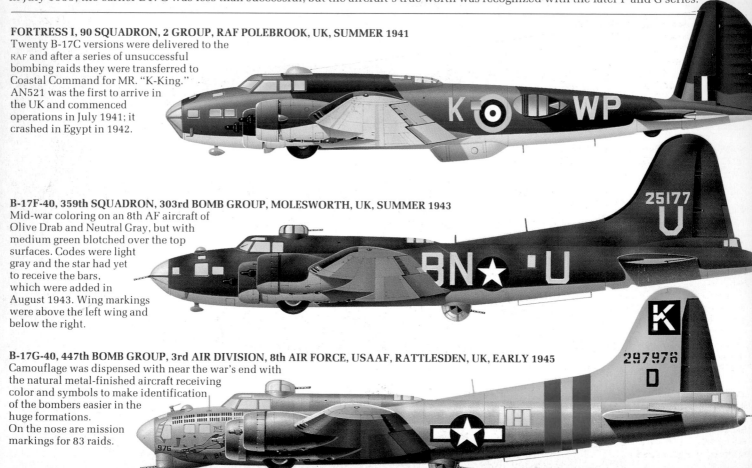

FORTRESS I, 90 SQUADRON, 2 GROUP, RAF POLEBROOK, UK, SUMMER 1941
Twenty B-17C versions were delivered to the RAF and after a series of unsuccessful bombing raids they were transferred to Coastal Command for MR. "K-King." AN521 was the first to arrive in the UK and commenced operations in July 1941; it crashed in Egypt in 1942.

B-17F-40, 359th SQUADRON, 303rd BOMB GROUP, MOLESWORTH, UK, SUMMER 1943
Mid-war coloring on an 8th AF aircraft of Olive Drab and Neutral Gray, but with medium green blotched over the top surfaces. Codes were light gray and the star had yet to receive the bars, which were added in August 1943. Wing markings were above the left wing and below the right.

B-17G-40, 447th BOMB GROUP, 3rd AIR DIVISION, 8th AIR FORCE, USAAF, RATTLESDEN, UK, EARLY 1945
Camouflage was dispensed with near the war's end with the natural metal-finished aircraft receiving color and symbols to make identification of the bombers easier in the huge formations.
On the nose are mission markings for 83 raids.

DORNIER Do 17

Medium-bomber/reconnaissance; 1700 manufactured; originally developed as a high-speed mailplane for Lufthansa, it was first used as a bomber by the Condor Legion during the Spanish Civil War; the 'Flying Pencil' was one of World War II's most famous bombers.

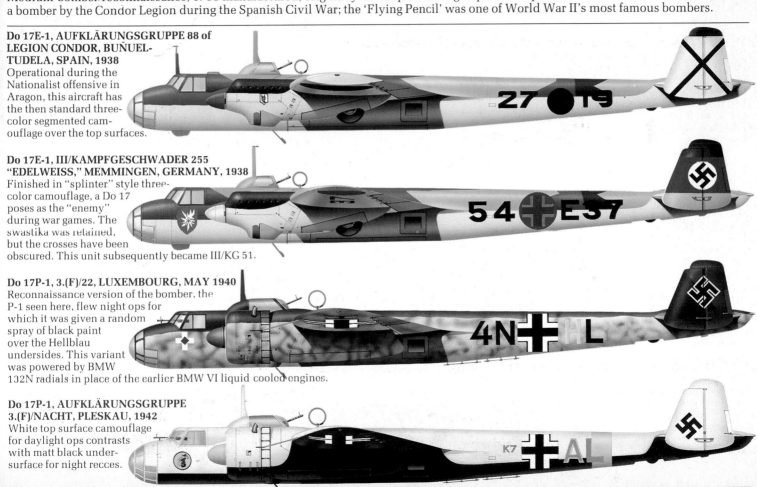

Do 17E-1, AUFKLÄRUNGSGRUPPE 88 of LEGION CONDOR, BUÑUEL-TUDELA, SPAIN, 1938
Operational during the Nationalist offensive in Aragon, this aircraft has the then standard three-color segmented camouflage over the top surfaces.

Do 17E-1, III/KAMPFGESCHWADER 255 "EDELWEISS," MEMMINGEN, GERMANY, 1938
Finished in "splinter" style three-color camouflage, a Do 17 poses as the "enemy" during war games. The swastika was retained, but the crosses have been obscured. This unit subsequently became III/KG 51.

Do 17P-1, 3.(F)/22, LUXEMBOURG, MAY 1940
Reconnaissance version of the bomber, the P-1 seen here, flew night ops for which it was given a random spray of black paint over the Hellblau undersides. This variant was powered by BMW 132N radials in place of the earlier BMW VI liquid cooled engines.

Do 17P-1, AUFKLÄRUNGSGRUPPE 3.(F)/NACHT, PLESKAU, 1942
White top surface camouflage for daylight ops contrasts with matt black undersurface for night recces.

MESSERSCHMITT Bf 109

Fighter; by 1939 C, D and E versions had been delivered – these were followed by the F, G and K series; 35,000 manufactured; the Bf 109 can claim to be the most produced fighter in history; Erich Hartmann had 352 victories flying 109s.

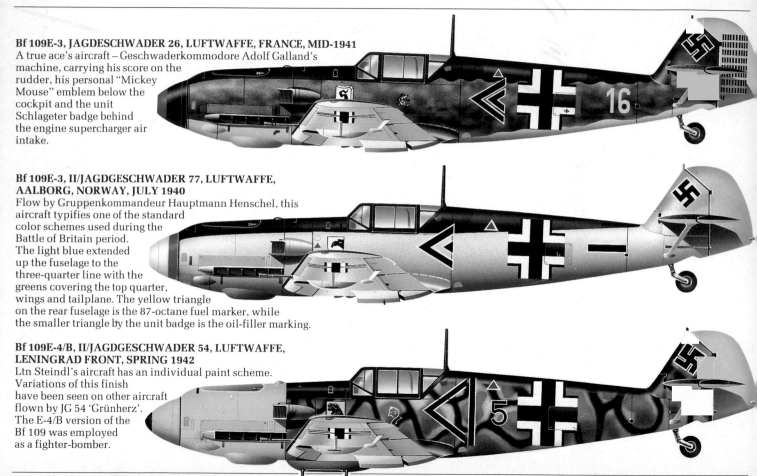

Bf 109E-3, JAGDESCHWADER 26, LUFTWAFFE, FRANCE, MID-1941
A true ace's aircraft – Geschwaderkommodore Adolf Galland's machine, carrying his score on the rudder, his personal "Mickey Mouse" emblem below the cockpit and the unit Schlageter badge behind the engine supercharger air intake.

Bf 109E-3, II/JAGDGESCHWADER 77, LUFTWAFFE, AALBORG, NORWAY, JULY 1940
Flow by Gruppenkommandeur Hauptmann Henschel, this aircraft typifies one of the standard color schemes used during the Battle of Britain period. The light blue extended up the fuselage to the three-quarter line with the greens covering the top quarter, wings and tailplane. The yellow triangle on the rear fuselage is the 87-octane fuel marker, while the smaller triangle by the unit badge is the oil-filler marking.

Bf 109E-4/B, II/JAGDGESCHWADER 54, LUFTWAFFE, LENINGRAD FRONT, SPRING 1942
Ltn Steindl's aircraft has an individual paint scheme. Variations of this finish have been seen on other aircraft flown by JG 54 'Grünherz'. The E-4/B version of the Bf 109 was employed as a fighter-bomber.

Bf 109-2/TROP, III/JAGDGESCHWADER 27, LUFTWAFFE, NORTH AFRICA, 1942
Considered the best of the breed, the F series refined the earlier E and became a true pilot's aircraft. In skilled hands it often defeated the cream of the Allied fighters, the Spitfire V. This Afrika Korps example has the unit badge on the nose and white Med. theater markings.

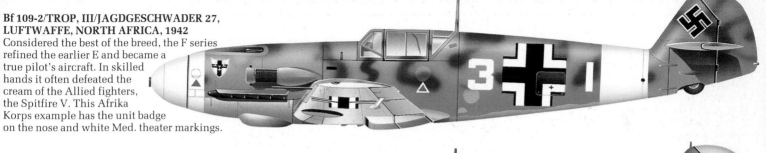

Bf 109F-4/B, 10.(JABO)/JAGDGESCHWADER 2, LUFTWAFFE, FRANCE, JUNE 1942
Staffelkapitan Oberleutnant Liesendahl flew this bomber version before being shot down on 17 July 1942 off Brixham, England. The red fox chewing a ship badge of JG2 "Richthofen" was painted on the nose, while the pilot's score of ships sunk or damaged was stenciled on the rudder.

Bf 109G-8, IV/JAGDGESCHWADER 5, LUFTWAFFE, FINLAND, WINTER 1943–4
One of the more unusual attempts at camouflage for operations during the winter months. In air-to-air combat, this dappled scheme was probably quite effective considering the snow/forest landscape against which most missions were flown.

FAIREY BATTLE

Bomber/trainer; designed to replace the Hawker Hart, the concept of the single-engined day bomber had been overtaken by technology by the outbreak of World War II; underpowered and underarmed, the Battle was withdrawn from frontline service in late 1940.

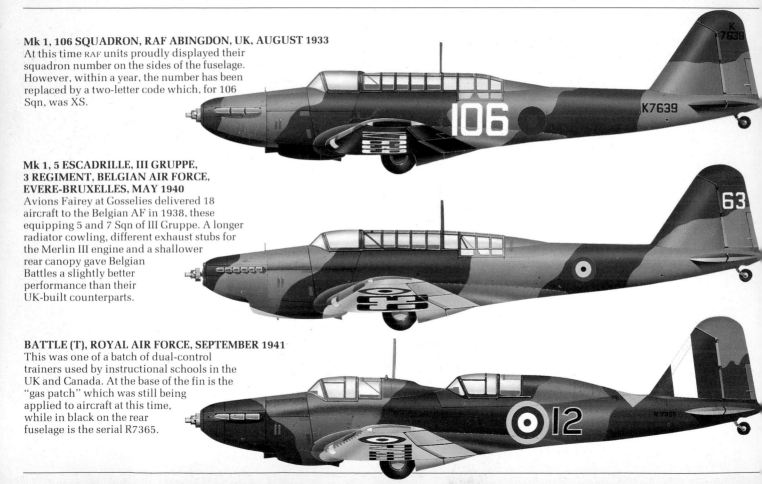

Mk 1, 106 SQUADRON, RAF ABINGDON, UK, AUGUST 1933
At this time RAF units proudly displayed their squadron number on the sides of the fuselage. However, within a year, the number has been replaced by a two-letter code which, for 106 Sqn, was XS.

Mk 1, 5 ESCADRILLE, III GRUPPE, 3 REGIMENT, BELGIAN AIR FORCE, EVERE-BRUXELLES, MAY 1940
Avions Fairey at Gosselies delivered 18 aircraft to the Belgian AF in 1938, these equipping 5 and 7 Sqn of III Gruppe. A longer radiator cowling, different exhaust stubs for the Merlin III engine and a shallower rear canopy gave Belgian Battles a slightly better performance than their UK-built counterparts.

BATTLE (T), ROYAL AIR FORCE, SEPTEMBER 1941
This was one of a batch of dual-control trainers used by instructional schools in the UK and Canada. At the base of the fin is the "gas patch" which was still being applied to aircraft at this time, while in black on the rear fuselage is the serial R7365.

Dive-bomber; the Stuka had a sinister appearance and at the outbreak of the war was used for propaganda but poor maneuverability and speed made it an easy target for the Allied fighters; its cranked wing and fixed wheel spats made it easy to identify.

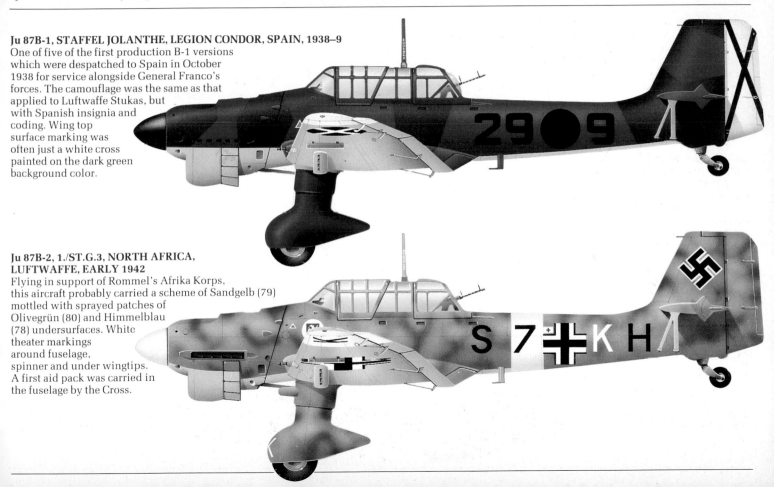

Ju 87B-1, STAFFEL JOLANTHE, LEGION CONDOR, SPAIN, 1938–9
One of five of the first production B-1 versions which were despatched to Spain in October 1938 for service alongside General Franco's forces. The camouflage was the same as that applied to Luftwaffe Stukas, but with Spanish insignia and coding. Wing top surface marking was often just a white cross painted on the dark green background color.

Ju 87B-2, 1./ST.G.3, NORTH AFRICA, LUFTWAFFE, EARLY 1942
Flying in support of Rommel's Afrika Korps, this aircraft probably carried a scheme of Sandgelb (79) mottled with sprayed patches of Olivegrün (80) and Himmelblau (78) undersurfaces. White theater markings around fuselage, spinner and under wingtips. A first aid pack was carried in the fuselage by the Cross.

FIESELER Fi 156 STORCH

Transport/communications/spotter; the Storch was able to land in almost the length of its wingspan and take off was nearly as impressive; it flew wherever the Wehrmacht fought; 2549 were manufactured and it was still operating in Vietnam in the 1950s.

Fi 156C-3/TROP, 2.(H)/14 AFRIKA KORPS, NORTH AFRICA, APRIL 1941
Tank spotting duties was the main task of this aircraft camouflaged in Sandgelb with Hellblau undersides. White areas under the outboard wing sections, around the fuselage and covering the rudder were a feature of North Africa-based aircraft. The unit's Edelweiss badge was painted on the engine cowling.

Fi 156C-3, KURIERSTAFFEL, LUFTWAFFE HIGH COMMAND, EASTERN FRONT, RUSSIA, 1942
As white was the identity marking in Africa, so yellow was the color applied to aircraft operating on the Russian Front. L2 was the code of Geschwaderstab of LG2, the letter B was the aircraft's code and A referred to the Staffel within the Geschwader.

Fi 156C-5, COMANDO AERONAUTICA ALBANIA (REGIA AERONAUTICA) ITALIAN AIR FORCE, TIRANA, ALBANIA, MARCH 1941
A number of Storch observation aircraft were supplied to the IAF and this example operating in Albania received a light green finish with gray undersides. The "fascis" emblem appears in front of the wide band.

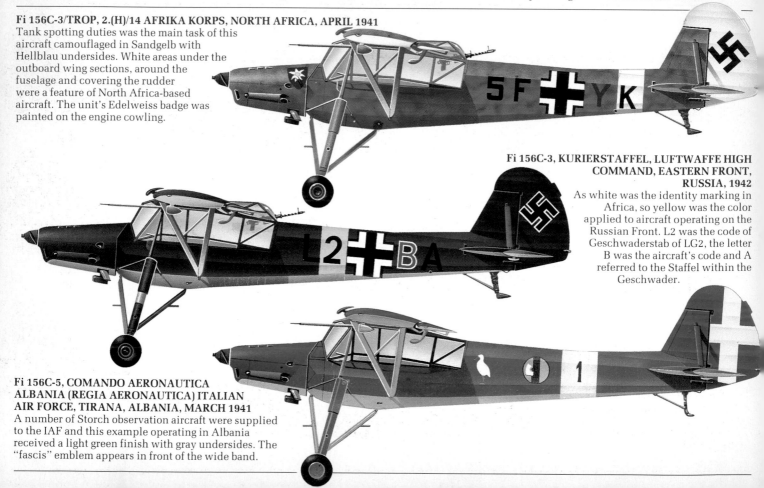

Bomber; built in Britain by the Bristol Co. and by Fairchild in Canada, where it was known as the Bolingbroke; more than 5000 manufactured; it differed in appearance to the Mk 1 having a longer nose but was equally unsuccessful in its daylight bombing role.

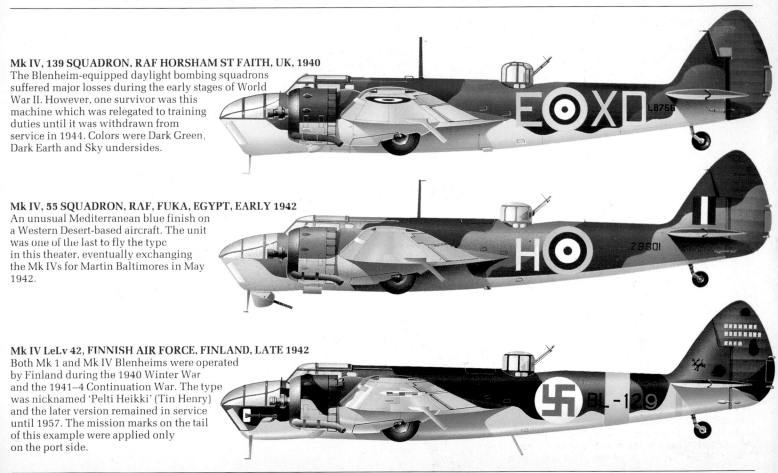

Mk IV, 139 SQUADRON, RAF HORSHAM ST FAITH, UK, 1940
The Blenheim-equipped daylight bombing squadrons suffered major losses during the early stages of World War II. However, one survivor was this machine which was relegated to training duties until it was withdrawn from service in 1944. Colors were Dark Green, Dark Earth and Sky undersides.

Mk IV, 55 SQUADRON, RAF, FUKA, EGYPT, EARLY 1942
An unusual Mediterranean blue finish on a Western Desert-based aircraft. The unit was one of the last to fly the type in this theater, eventually exchanging the Mk IVs for Martin Baltimores in May 1942.

Mk IV LeLv 42, FINNISH AIR FORCE, FINLAND, LATE 1942
Both Mk 1 and Mk IV Blenheims were operated by Finland during the 1940 Winter War and the 1941–4 Continuation War. The type was nicknamed 'Pelti Heikki' (Tin Henry) and the later version remained in service until 1957. The mission marks on the tail of this example were applied only on the port side.

A.W. WHITLEY

Heavy bomber; first of the trio (others were the Wellington and Hampden) with which RAF went to war in 1939; with a top speed of only 192mph at 14,300 feet, was used solely for night operations; range extended to northern Italy from Britain.

Mk IV, 10 SQUADRON, RAF DISHFORTH, UK, 1938
After 1939 the PB squadron code was changed to ZA, Underwing white serials were 45in high, and the fuselage serials, 8in high. The serial number is repeated on the rudder fin.

Mk V, 78 SQUADRON, RAF DISHFORTH, UK, 1941
In this all-black version the original Type A1 roundel has been modified to a C1 and the individual aircraft letter (Y) has been made more prominent. The serials are now white and placed on the fuselage.

Mk V, RAF, 1942
Retired from bomber operations in the spring of 1942, Whitleys undertook other duties including leaflet, supply and agent dropping. This uncoded Mk V is painted in the official temperate land camouflage scheme of World War II. Its serial is painted black.

Mk VII, 502 SQUADRON, RAF ST EVAL, UK, 1941
From 10 August 1941 all RAF Coastal Command Whitleys (and other types) were ordered to be given white undersurfaces and sides with Dark Slate Gray and Extra Dark Sea Gray on surfaces viewed from immediately above.

VOUGHT SB2U VINDICATOR

Carrier based scout-bomber; a cantilever monoplane equipped with folding outer wings for ship stowage; impressive during trials in 1936, its combat career was brief, a courageous action against the Japanese at Midway finally confirming its obsolescence.

SB2U-1, COMMANDER RANGER AIR GROUP, US NAVY, USS *RANGER*, 1940
In 1940 three units – VB-4, VS-41 and VS-42 – were equipped with SB2Us aboard this carrier, green tails identifying aircraft attached to the ship. With America still neutral, the aircraft displayed a neutrality patrol star on the engine cowling. The black stripes on the fin are landing assistance lines for carrier use.

SB2U-1, VS-41, US NAVY, USS *RANGER*, AUGUST 1942
The red center had been deleted from the national insignia by this time and the aircraft itself was about to depart from the front-line scene as the USN accepted that it was not up to the combat standards of the time. The Non-Specular Blue Gray top surface color was also applied to the underside of the outer folding wing panels.

CHESAPEAKE 1, 811 SQUADRON, ROYAL NAVY, LEE-ON-SOLENT, UK, AUTUMN 1941
The British, too, ordered the type and 50 were delivered, but their performance was not considered good enough for front-line use. Color scheme was Dark Slate Gray (a gray-green color) and Extra Dark Sea Gray with Sky undersides.

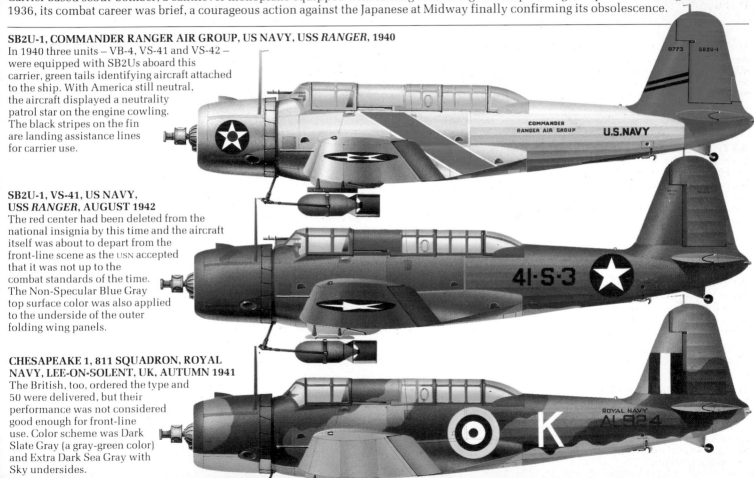

FOCKE-WULF Fw 200

Bomber/transport; a 26-passenger airliner developed into a long-distance commerce raider; achieved some success before the advent of long-range Coastal Command aircraft and catapult armed merchantmen fighters eliminated its threat; a total of 276 were built.

Fw 200V3, "IMMELMANN III," REGIERUNGSSTAFFEL, BERLIN, GERMANY, 1940

Hitler's personal transport received the standard bomber camouflage finish of Schwarzgrün and Dunkelgrün with Hellblau undersides. Hitler's compartment featured a large armoured seat placed over an escape hatch and incorporated a parachute pack. The 26-00 code was previously used on the Führer's Ju 52s.

Fw 200C-0, 1/KG 40, LUFTWAFFE, STALINGRAD, USSR, JANUARY 1943

Supply flights to the beleaguered 6th Army found large numbers of aircraft impressed into the operation, including this armed transport version which received a coat of "winter white" over the dark green upper surfaces. It was normally attached to the Reich Air Ministry Pool based at Berlin-Staaken.

Fw 200C-8, III/KG 40, LUFTWAFFE, BORDEAUX-MARIGNAC, FRANCE, 1944

The last production variant was equipped with FuG 200 Hohentwiel search radar in the nose and a Henschel Hs293 anti-ship missile under each wing. Few successes were achieved by this combination and the type reverted to its original role – that of transportation.

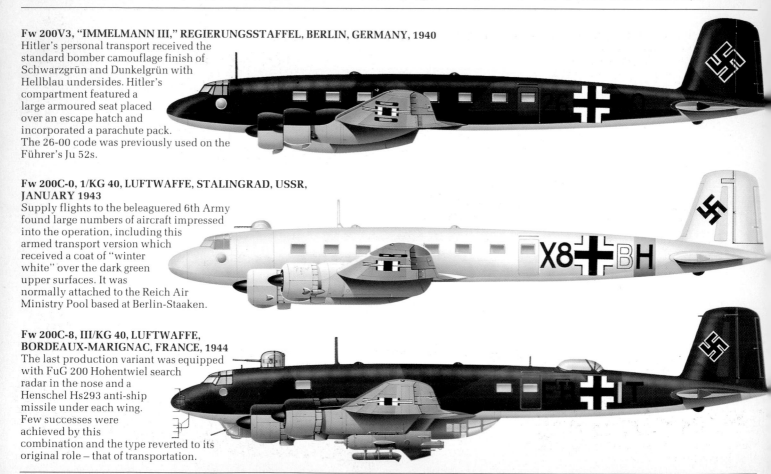

MORANE-SAULNIER M.S.406

Fighter; 860-hp Hispano-Suiza engine; one 20mm cannon and two 7.5mm machine guns; 573 manufactured. Although sturdy and highly maneuverable, the M.S.406 was too slow and insufficiently-armed to combat the Luftwaffe's Bf 109.

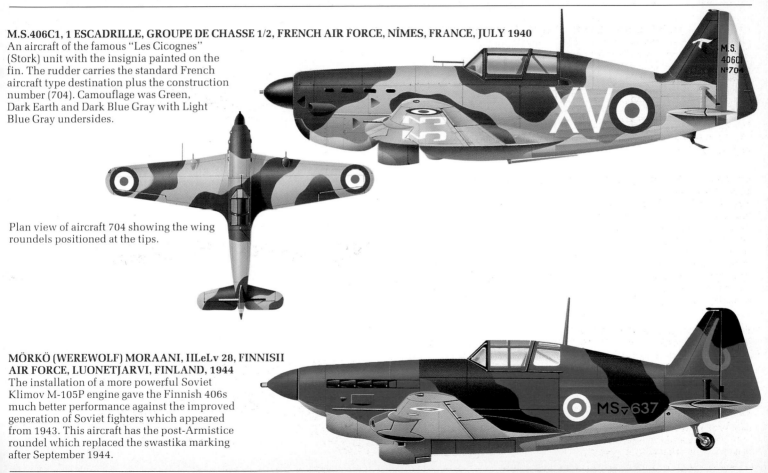

M.S.406C1, 1 ESCADRILLE, GROUPE DE CHASSE 1/2, FRENCH AIR FORCE, NÎMES, FRANCE, JULY 1940
An aircraft of the famous "Les Cicognes" (Stork) unit with the insignia painted on the fin. The rudder carries the standard French aircraft type destination plus the construction number (704). Camouflage was Green, Dark Earth and Dark Blue Gray with Light Blue Gray undersides.

Plan view of aircraft 704 showing the wing roundels positioned at the tips.

MÖRKÖ (WEREWOLF) MORAANI, IILeLv 28, FINNISII AIR FORCE, LUONETJARVI, FINLAND, 1944
The installation of a more powerful Soviet Klimov M-105P engine gave the Finnish 406s much better performance against the improved generation of Soviet fighters which appeared from 1943. This aircraft has the post-Armistice roundel which replaced the swastika marking after September 1944.

SUPERMARINE SPITFIRE

Fighter; engines and armaments varied through 32 marks (24 Spitfire, 8 Seafire); 20, 351 Spitfires and 2556 Seafires manufactured (the Seafire was a carrier-based version of the Spitfire); the Spitfire fought on every front and finally retired from service on 1st April 1954.

Mk I, 19 SQUADRON, RAF DUXFORD, UK, OCTOBER 1938

One of the first RAF Spitfires delivered, carrying the soon-to-be-deleted unit number on the fin. The camouflage is Dark Green, Dark Earth disruptive pattern. The plane displays 56in upper-surface wing roundels, 35in Type A1 fuselage roundels and 50in underwing roundels.

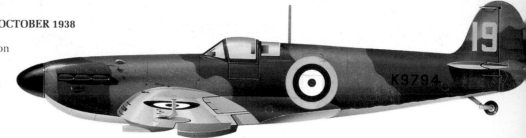

Mk IIb, 306 (POLISH) SQUADRON, RAF NORTHOLT, UK, AUGUST 1941

This was the month Fighter Command changed its colors from Dark Green, Dark Earth to Dark Green, Ocean Gray to reflect offensive operations which were getting underway at that time. Medium Sea Gray is now painted on the undersides. The badge on the nose is of the Polish Torunski unit.

Mk Vb, 40 SQUADRON, SOUTH AFRICAN AIR FORCE, ITALY, AUGUST 1943

Dark Earth and Middle Stone with Azure Blue undersides was a scheme found to be ideal in the Middle East. This machine has an Aboukir tropical filter under the nose and a camera port in the rear fuselage.

Mk Vc, 308th FIGHTER SQUADRON, 31st FG, USAAF, TUNISIA, 1943
Another variation of the ME scheme on an aircraft deployed for the Torch landings in North Africa. Note the different type of tropical sand filter under the nose compared with the previous machine.

Mk IX, 402 SQUADRON, ROYAL CANADIAN AIR FORCE, KENLEY, UK, 1943
Fighter Command's day fighter scheme for the mid-war years. For quick identification in combat, the Sky spinner and fuselage band were supplemented by yellow leading edges to the wings. Unit badge under cockpit.

Mk 22, 603 (CITY OF EDINBURGH) SQUADRON, R AUX AF, TURNHOUSE, UK, 1950
Post-war the RAF promulgated an order for a return to the silver finish of pre-1939. This unit was initially allocated RAF codes, but these were later changed to XT when the unit transferred from Reserve status to Fighter Command; "Q" is the individual aircraft letter.

MESSERSCHMITT Bf 110

Fighter; twin engined and conceived by the Luftwaffe as the long-range element of its fighter arm but proved unable to hold its own against single seat fighters; performed far more effectively as a night-fighter; 6,050 were built.

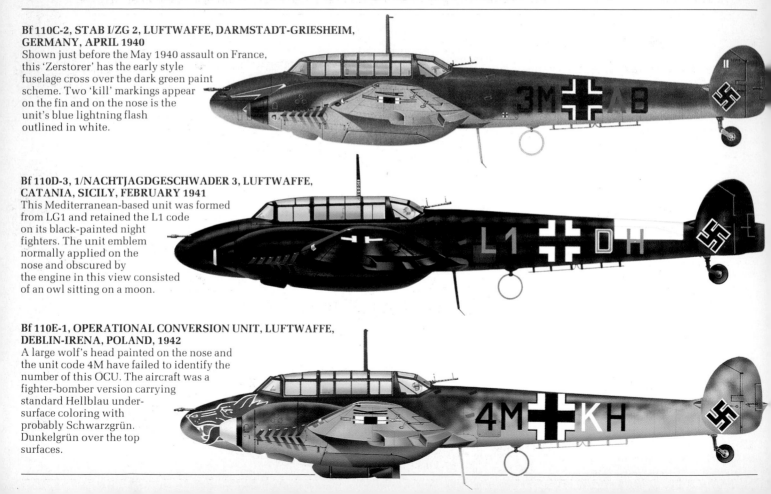

Bf 110C-2, STAB I/ZG 2, LUFTWAFFE, DARMSTADT-GRIESHEIM, GERMANY, APRIL 1940

Shown just before the May 1940 assault on France, this 'Zerstorer' has the early style fuselage cross over the dark green paint scheme. Two 'kill' markings appear on the fin and on the nose is the unit's blue lightning flash outlined in white.

Bf 110D-3, 1/NACHTJAGDGESCHWADER 3, LUFTWAFFE, CATANIA, SICILY, FEBRUARY 1941

This Mediterranean-based unit was formed from LG1 and retained the L1 code on its black-painted night fighters. The unit emblem normally applied on the nose and obscured by the engine in this view consisted of an owl sitting on a moon.

Bf 110E-1, OPERATIONAL CONVERSION UNIT, LUFTWAFFE, DEBLIN-IRENA, POLAND, 1942

A large wolf's head painted on the nose and the unit code 4M have failed to identify the number of this OCU. The aircraft was a fighter-bomber version carrying standard Hellblau under-surface coloring with probably Schwarzgrün. Dunkelgrün over the top surfaces.

Medium-range reconnaissance/bomber; designed to an RAF Coastal Command requirement, it was derived from the Super-Electra liner to which was added a bomb-bay, gun turret, forward firing guns in the nose and other military equipment; 2584 were built.

A-29, US ARMY AIR CORPS, EARLY 1942
Built for the RAF as a Hudson Mk IIIA but repossessed by USAAC for ASW patrols. British Dark Green, Dark Earth camouflage was retained. The Red in the star was removed from May 1942 after the US entered World War II. The RAF black serial was retained under the tail.

Mk V, 48 SQUADRON, RAF STORNOWAY, SCOTLAND, 1941
This Temperate Sea Scheme was ordered for all Hudsons and other RAF Coastal Command landplanes. Night (matt Black) undersides were carried for nocturnal bombing missions. Note the earlier roundels and rudder stripes compared with these on OS-T below.

Mk VI, RAF, 1943
An uncoded Hudson armed with underwing rockets. This weapon was used successfully by aircraft of 608 Sqn against U-boats in the Mediterranean.

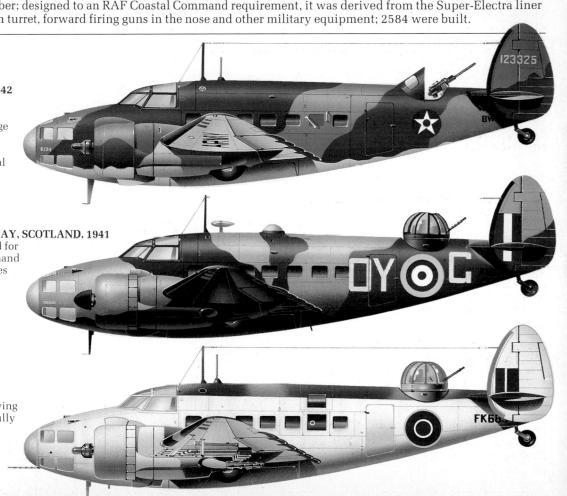

DOUGLAS A-20 BOSTON

Bomber; the prototype first flew in August 1939 and France was the first overseas customer; the DB-7 had a respectable top speed of 314 mph; for the night intruder and fighter role, was known as the Havoc; 7385 were produced.

DB-7B, GROUPE DE BOMBARDEMENT 1/19, ARMÉE-DE-L'AIR DE L'ARMISTICE, BLIDA, ALGERIA, AUTUMN 1940

The 24th production aircraft, this DB-7 carries the early special marking applied at this time to all Vichy-operated aircraft: a white horizontal stripe along the fuselage and a white outer circle to the fuselage roundel. Camouflage was Dark Green, Light Earth and Blue-Gray upper surfaces with Light Blue-Gray undersides.

HAVOC Mk 1, 23 SQUADRON, RAF, FORD, UK, APRIL 1941

Operated on intruder sorties from the south of England, BD112 is finished in overall Special Night RDM 2A (black) with Sky Gray codes and Dull Red serial. Fuselage roundel is a Type A1, while above the wings they were Type B.

A-20B, 47th BOMB GROUP, USAAF, SOUK-EL-ARBA, TUNISIA, MAY 1943

Desert Sand was the official camouflage for USAAF aircraft in this theater, and this pristine example contrasts with many which had various combinations of Olive Drab, Dark Green and Brown schemes. The large tail numbers were sometimes hand-painted crudely.

CONSOLIDATED PBY CATALINA

Flying-boat patrol/bomber; long endurance was the main requirement for this fine twin-engined flying boat; served reliably throughout World War II in almost every theater; main versions were the PBY-5,-5A and -6; 3,281 were built in the USA and Canada.

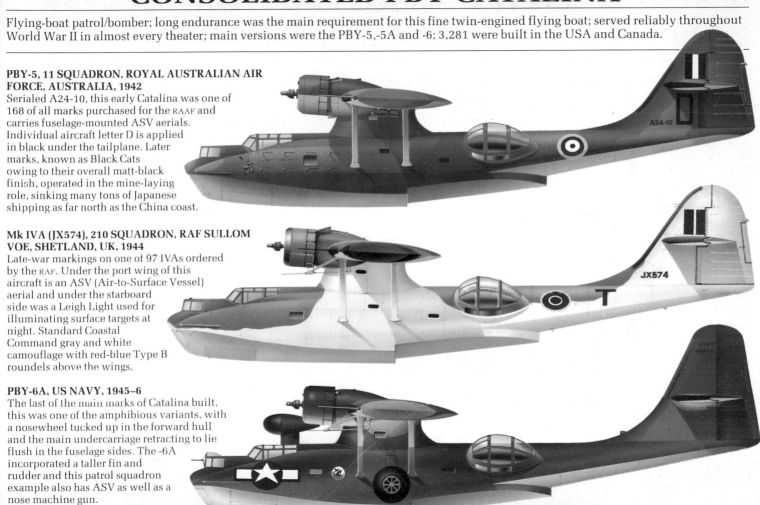

PBY-5, 11 SQUADRON, ROYAL AUSTRALIAN AIR FORCE, AUSTRALIA, 1942

Serialed A24-10, this early Catalina was one of 168 of all marks purchased for the RAAF and carries fuselage-mounted ASV aerials. Individual aircraft letter D is applied in black under the tailplane. Later marks, known as Black Cats owing to their overall matt-black finish, operated in the mine-laying role, sinking many tons of Japanese shipping as far north as the China coast.

Mk IVA (JX574), 210 SQUADRON, RAF SULLOM VOE, SHETLAND, UK, 1944

Late-war markings on one of 97 IVAs ordered by the RAF. Under the port wing of this aircraft is an ASV (Air-to-Surface Vessel) aerial and under the starboard side was a Leigh Light used for illuminating surface targets at night. Standard Coastal Command gray and white camouflage with red-blue Type B roundels above the wings.

PBY-6A, US NAVY, 1945–6

The last of the main marks of Catalina built, this was one of the amphibious variants, with a nosewheel tucked up in the forward hull and the main undercarriage retracting to lie flush in the fuselage sides. The -6A incorporated a taller fin and rudder and this patrol squadron example also has ASV as well as a nose machine gun.

BOULTON PAUL DEFIANT

Night fighter; lack of forward armament proved a major weakness in daylight combat and true potential only realized when this two-seater switched to night-fighting; the Defiant Mk I and II differed mainly in engine power, while the Mk III was used as a tug.

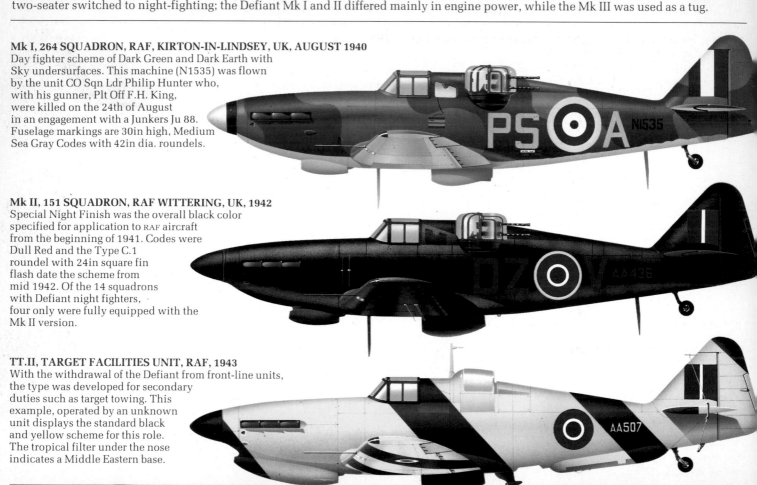

Mk I, 264 SQUADRON, RAF, KIRTON-IN-LINDSEY, UK, AUGUST 1940
Day fighter scheme of Dark Green and Dark Earth with Sky undersurfaces. This machine (N1535) was flown by the unit CO Sqn Ldr Philip Hunter who, with his gunner, Plt Off F.H. King, were killed on the 24th of August in an engagement with a Junkers Ju 88. Fuselage markings are 30in high, Medium Sea Gray Codes with 42in dia. roundels.

Mk II, 151 SQUADRON, RAF WITTERING, UK, 1942
Special Night Finish was the overall black color specified for application to RAF aircraft from the beginning of 1941. Codes were Dull Red and the Type C.1 roundel with 24in square fin flash date the scheme from mid 1942. Of the 14 squadrons with Defiant night fighters, four only were fully equipped with the Mk II version.

TT.II, TARGET FACILITIES UNIT, RAF, 1943
With the withdrawal of the Defiant from front-line units, the type was developed for secondary duties such as target towing. This example, operated by an unknown unit displays the standard black and yellow scheme for this role. The tropical filter under the nose indicates a Middle Eastern base.

JUNKERS Ju 88

Bomber/night-fighter/reconnaissance; the most versatile of all Germany's 1939-45 airplanes; the Ju88 V1 first flew in December 1936 and production aircraft joined the first unit early in 1939; nearly 15,000 had been built by the end of the war.

Ju 88A-5, III/LEHRGESCHWADER 1, X FLIEGERKORPS, LUFTWAFFE, SICILY, 1941
Standard finish for bombers of this period before improvization by the units took hold and more disruptive schemes appeared. LG1 operated from Catania, mainly on anti-shipping operations around Malta between May 1941 and May 1942. White theater band around fuselage only.

Ju 88A-10, II/LEHRGESCHWADER 1, LUFTWAFFE, CRETE, OCTOBER 1942
Hastily redeployed from North African operations to anti-shipping duties in Crete, this tropicalized version of the A-5 bomber retains its desert camouflage until an extended maintenance check is needed and a more appropriate color scheme can be applied.

Ju 88G-7a, IV/NACHTJAGDGESCHWADER 6, LUFTWAFFE, SCHWÄBISCH HALL, GERMANY, 1944–5
A light gray finish was adopted by Luftwaffe night fighters. Markings were usually black or dark gray and on this aircraft the tail has been painted to resemble that of the lower performance Ju 88C variant.

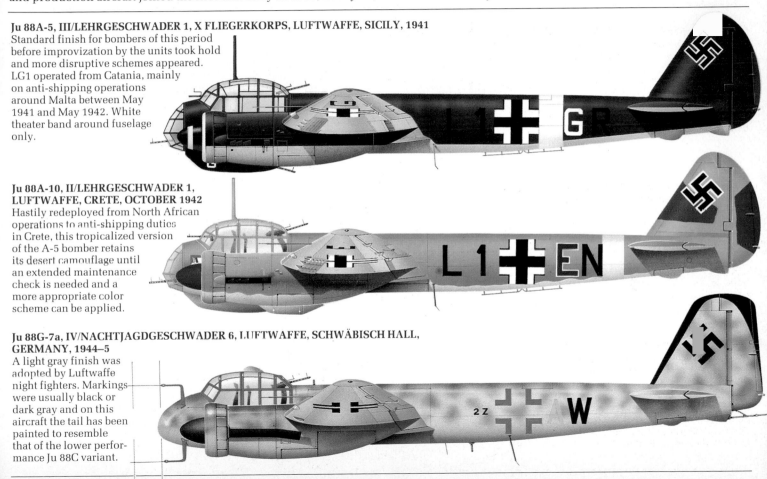

FIAT CR.42

Fighter; probably the best of the biplane fighters but it stood little chance against faster, more heavily armed monoplanes such as the Hurricane; it was ordered by Belgium, Hungary and Sweden as well as the Regia Aeronautica and production totalled 1781.

CR.42, 83 SQUADRIGLIA, 18 GRUPPO, 3 STORMO, LIBYA, EARLY 1941
Dark Green and Red-Brown over the Yellow Ocher was another desert scheme used on Italian fighters, and it was retained by this unit during its brief series of operations in 1940 against the UK when based in Belgium. A Cmdte pennant is painted under the cockpit, and the dark stripe on the rear fuselage is an overpainted white marking used in Belgium.

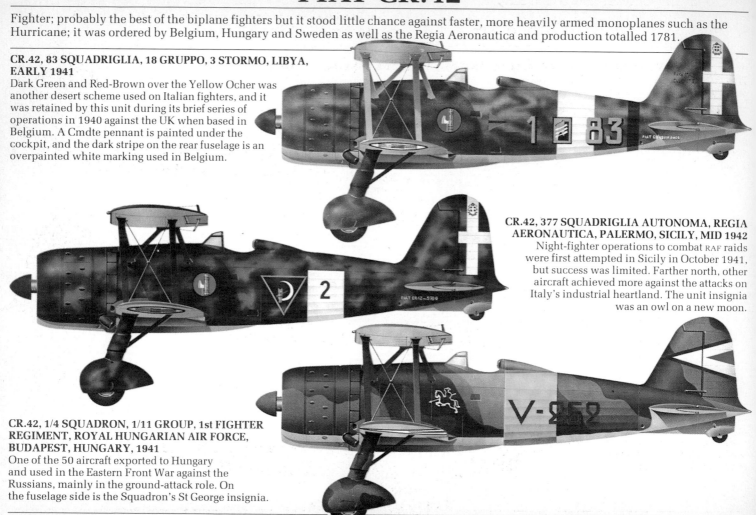

CR.42, 377 SQUADRIGLIA AUTONOMA, REGIA AERONAUTICA, PALERMO, SICILY, MID 1942
Night-fighter operations to combat RAF raids were first attempted in Sicily in October 1941, but success was limited. Farther north, other aircraft achieved more against the attacks on Italy's industrial heartland. The unit insignia was an owl on a new moon.

CR.42, 1/4 SQUADRON, 1/11 GROUP, 1st FIGHTER REGIMENT, ROYAL HUNGARIAN AIR FORCE, BUDAPEST, HUNGARY, 1941
One of the 50 aircraft exported to Hungary and used in the Eastern Front War against the Russians, mainly in the ground-attack role. On the fuselage side is the Squadron's St George insignia.

Carrier-based fighter; heavily involved in the 7 December 1941 raid on Pearl Harbor; marks were also known as Reisen or Zeke and the A6M3 as Hamp, however, to most people it was known as the Zero; 10,450 were built by the war's end.

A6M2, AIRCRAFT CARRIER *HIRYU*, IMPERIAL JAPANESE NAVY, PEARL HARBOR, DECEMBER 1941
This machine was part of the attacking force on the "day of infamy." Overall scheme was Light Gray (N10), with blue signifying the Second Air Division, the two stripes indicating the second ship. The tail code BII also meant the same (B=2nd AD, II=2nd ship).

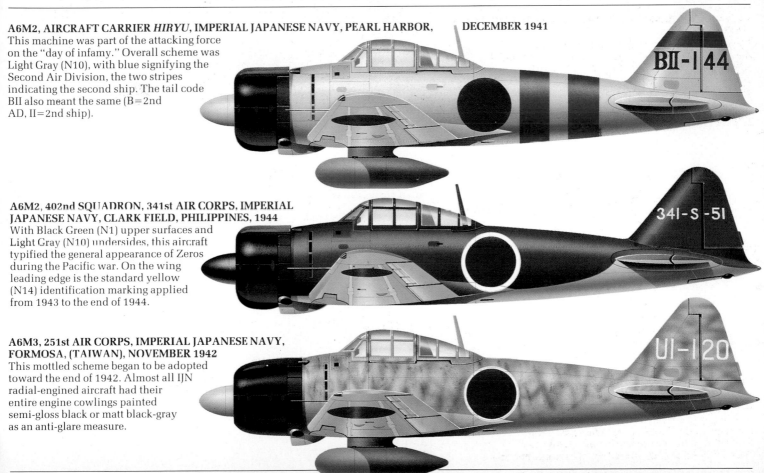

A6M2, 402nd SQUADRON, 341st AIR CORPS, IMPERIAL JAPANESE NAVY, CLARK FIELD, PHILIPPINES, 1944
With Black Green (N1) upper surfaces and Light Gray (N10) undersides, this aircraft typified the general appearance of Zeros during the Pacific war. On the wing leading edge is the standard yellow (N14) identification marking applied from 1943 to the end of 1944.

A6M3, 251st AIR CORPS, IMPERIAL JAPANESE NAVY, FORMOSA, (TAIWAN), NOVEMBER 1942
This mottled scheme began to be adopted toward the end of 1942. Almost all IJN radial-engined aircraft had their entire engine cowlings painted semi-gloss black or matt black-gray as an anti-glare measure.

BRISTOL BEAUFIGHTER

Long-range heavy fighter; four 20mm cannons in belly, six .303 in machine guns in wings; max speed of 321mph at 15,800 ft; the Beaufighter used 75 per cent Beaufort bomber components and operated in most theaters in World War II, surviving until 1960.

Mk 1F, 25 SQUADRON, RAF NORTH WEALD, UK, 1940
This aircraft carries standard day fighter colors of Dark Green, Dark Earth and Sky undersurfaces. It has 35in diameter Type A1 fuselage roundels and 45in diameter Type A underwing roundels. 25 Sqn was, with 29 Sqn, the first unit to receive Beaufighters.

Mk II 307 (POLISH) SQUADRON, RAF EXETER, UK, 1941
It has overall Special Night (RDM2) matt black finish, dull Red codes, serial and badge, 24×27in fin flash and 35in diameter fuselage roundel.

Mk TT10, 34 SQUADRON, RAF, 1950's
This final Beaufighter variant has a natural metal finish. It was employed on anti-aircraft cooperation duties, and the diagonal black and yellow stripes on the undersides of the wing denote its role as a target tug. The last example was withdrawn from service in 1960.

GRUMMAN AVENGER

Torpedo-bomber; despite losing five of the six aircraft despatched during the battle of Midway in June 1942, survived in service to become one of the outstanding torpedo bombers of World War II; greatly modified, it continued in use until the 1960s.

TBF-1, VT-8, US NAVY, MIDWAY, HAWAIIAN ISLANDS, USA, 4 JUNE 1942
One of the five aircraft shot down during the Avenger's first combat sortie. At this time the colors were Non-specular Blue Gray over all top surfaces and fuselage sides, with Non-specular Light Gray on the undersurfaces.

TBM-3, US NAVY, USS *RANDOLPH* (CV-15), TASK FORCE 58, EARLY 1944
Standard three-tone camouflage for the mid-war period (see the Hellcat for colors), with white stripes denoting the carrier and the aircraft number on the fuselage and nose. As an alternative to the single 22in torpedo, the Avenger's internal bomb-bay could carry up to 2,000lb of bombs or mines.

AVENGER Mk II, ROYAL NAVY, RNAS DONIBRISTLE, UK, MID 1944
Invasion bands circle the fuselage and wings of an aircraft with a fox head insignia under the cockpit, but there is little else to identify it apart from the partly obscured serial JZ490 on the dorsal fin. The RN received more than 950 Avengers, calling them Tarpons until January 1944.

HENSCHEL Hs 129

Tank buster; two Argus in-line engines, later unreliable Gnome-Rhone 14Ms; intended to replace the Ju 87D as a tank buster using light bombs and a heavy caliber cannon but never achieved the reliability required; production terminated in 1944 after 866 had been built.

Hs 129B-1, 4./SCH.G.2, LUFTWAFFE, LIBYA, NOVEMBER 1942
This unit was formed in Poland in September 1942 with 12 machines. By the time it reached North Africa its strength was reduced to eight, of which half were unserviceable. The fuselage marking indicates the pilot was the Gruppe Technical Officer.

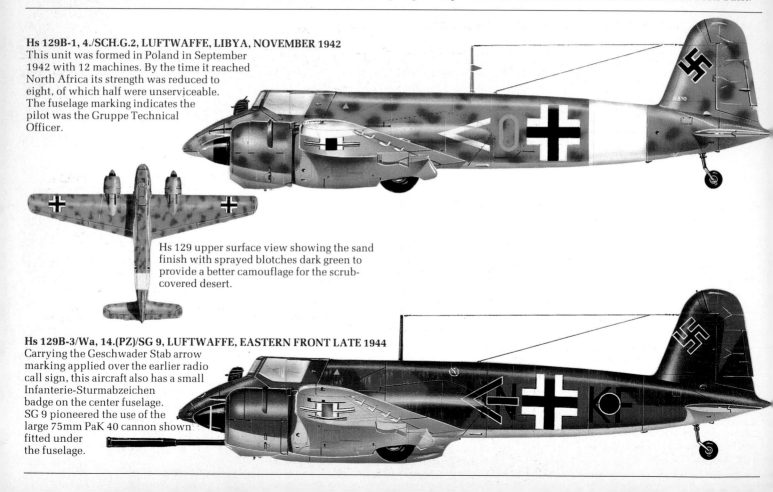

Hs 129 upper surface view showing the sand finish with sprayed blotches dark green to provide a better camouflage for the scrub-covered desert.

Hs 129B-3/Wa, 14.(PZ)/SG 9, LUFTWAFFE, EASTERN FRONT LATE 1944
Carrying the Geschwader Stab arrow marking applied over the earlier radio call sign, this aircraft also has a small Infanterie-Sturmabzeichen badge on the center fuselage. SG 9 pioneered the use of the large 75mm PaK 40 cannon shown fitted under the fuselage.

CURTISS HAWK

Fighter; replacing the air-cooled radial engine of the Hawk 75 with a liquid-cooled powerplant produced the Hawk 81 series of famous P-40s and RAF-operated Tomahawks which were sluggish in performance but extremely rugged.

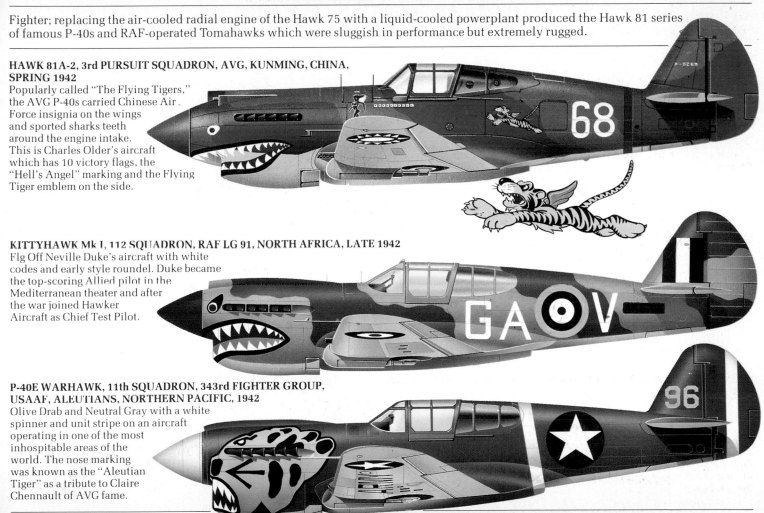

HAWK 81A-2, 3rd PURSUIT SQUADRON, AVG, KUNMING, CHINA, SPRING 1942
Popularly called "The Flying Tigers," the AVG P-40s carried Chinese Air Force insignia on the wings and sported sharks teeth around the engine intake. This is Charles Older's aircraft which has 10 victory flags, the "Hell's Angel" marking and the Flying Tiger emblem on the side.

KITTYHAWK Mk I, 112 SQUADRON, RAF LG 91, NORTH AFRICA, LATE 1942
Flg Off Neville Duke's aircraft with white codes and early style roundel. Duke became the top-scoring Allied pilot in the Mediterranean theater and after the war joined Hawker Aircraft as Chief Test Pilot.

P-40E WARHAWK, 11th SQUADRON, 343rd FIGHTER GROUP, USAAF, ALEUTIANS, NORTHERN PACIFIC, 1942
Olive Drab and Neutral Gray with a white spinner and unit stripe on an aircraft operating in one of the most inhospitable areas of the world. The nose marking was known as the "Aleutian Tiger" as a tribute to Claire Chennault of AVG fame.

BLOHM UND VOSS Bv 138

Reconnaissance, SAR, mine-sweeping, anti-shipping flying boat; nicknamed the 'flying clog' by the Luftwaffe because of the shape of the central hull, the 3-engined Bv138 was a remarkably efficient flying boat; the 'C' was the major production type; production totaled 279.

C-1, 2./KÜSTENFLIEGERGRUPPEN 406, LUFTWAFFE, NORWAY, 1942
The standard finish on flying-boats reflected the general Luftwaffe color scheme, that of Dunkelgrün (dark green), Schwartzgrün (black-green) with Hellblau (clear blue) undersides. This example was employed against the Arctic Convoy PQ 13 taking war supplies to the Soviet Union.

C-1/U1, 1.(F)/SAGr 130, LUFTWAFFE, TRONDHEIM AREA, NORWAY, APRIL 1944
During operations in the Arctic Ocean aircraft were often given a random application of white paint to enable them to merge better with the ice floes on reconnaissance missions. The aircraft were refuelled from U-boats to extend their range.

MS (MINENSUCHE), 6./MSGr.1, LUFTWAFFE, GROSSENBRODE, BALTIC SEA, 1944–5
Dubbed the *Mouse-catching aircraft* owing to the circular de-gaussing ring for mine sweeping, these modified machines had the auxiliary motor for energizing the ring mounted in place of the front turret.

SHORT SUNDERLAND

Long-range maritime reconnaissance flying boat; powered by Bristol Pegasus engines, later Pratt & Whitney Twin Wasps (for Mark V); had up to 12 machine guns in addition to bombs and depth charges; 752 were manufactured including 31 Mark IVs (called Seafords)

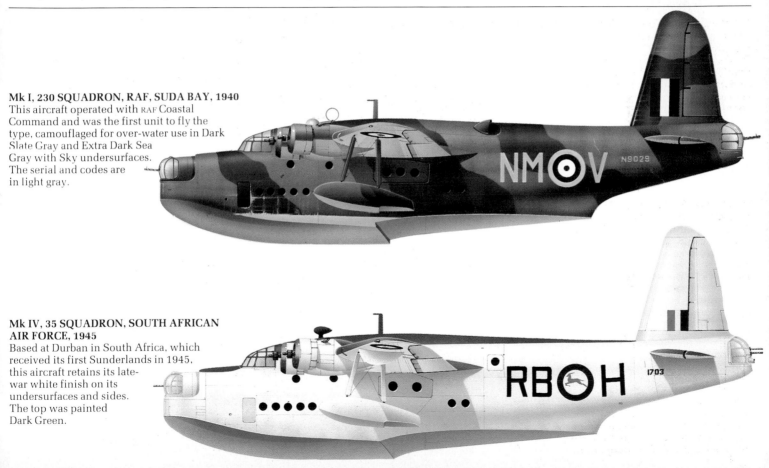

Mk I, 230 SQUADRON, RAF, SUDA BAY, 1940
This aircraft operated with RAF Coastal Command and was the first unit to fly the type, camouflaged for over-water use in Dark Slate Gray and Extra Dark Sea Gray with Sky undersurfaces. The serial and codes are in light gray.

Mk IV, 35 SQUADRON, SOUTH AFRICAN AIR FORCE, 1945
Based at Durban in South Africa, which received its first Sunderlands in 1945, this aircraft retains its late-war white finish on its undersurfaces and sides. The top was painted Dark Green.

BREWSTER BUFFALO

Fighter; the US Navy's first shipborne fighter monoplane; flown in prototype in 1937 and clearly superior to the biplanes it replaced this tubby design was shown by the experience of Midway to be no match for the Japanese Zeros.

F2A-2, VF-2 "FLYING CHIEFS," US NAVY, USS *LEXINGTON*, MARCH 1941
While Europe was fighting it out, America's armed forces still maintained their peacetime appearances, as shown by this machine. It was painted with two different yellows: glossy chrome above the upper wing surfaces and lemon yellow on the cowling, fuselage and tail unit – the latter denoting *Lexington*.

F2A-3, VMF-221, US MARINE CORPS, EWA, HAWAIIAN ISLANDS, MID-1942
Part of the defenses of Pearl Harbor, this unit removed the red circle in the star and the rudder striping on 15 May 1942. The camouflage was Non-Specular Blue Gray and Light Gray.

DOUGLAS DAUNTLESS

Carrier-based dive-bomber; developed in the mid-1930s for US Navy; relatively slow and outmoded when it began its combat career in 1942, it was rugged and dependable and on giving way to the Helldiver had sunk more Japanese ships than any other aircraft.

SBD-1, VMSB-232 (EX-VMB-2), US MARINE CORPS AIR GROUP 21, HAWAIIAN ISLANDS, DECEMBER 1941
When the Japanese struck Oahu on 7 December 1941 they caught the Dauntlesses of Marine Air Group 21 on the ground and badly battered them. At the time these early SBD-1s were finished in the Non-Specular Light Gray as directed by a 30 December 1940 order.

SBD-4, VMSB-243, 1st MARINE AIR WING, MUNDA, NEW GEORGIA, SOLOMON ISLANDS, AUGUST 1943
Wearing the short-lived red-bordered insignia, this Marine aircraft carries a 500lb 'calling card' under the fuselage.

A-24B GROUPE DE CHASSE-BOMBARDEMENT (GCB) 1/18 "VENDÉE," VANNES FRANCE, NOV 1944
Olive Drab and Neutral Gray colors overpainted with invasion stripes and, in this case, a large Free French Cross of Lorraine.

NAKAJIMA Ki-49 DONRYU

Heavy bomber; under-powered bomber operated by the Japanese Army Air Force; defensive armament consisted of 12 .7mm machine guns in nose, tail, ventral and beam positions, plus a single 20mm cannon in the dorsal position; more than 800 were built.

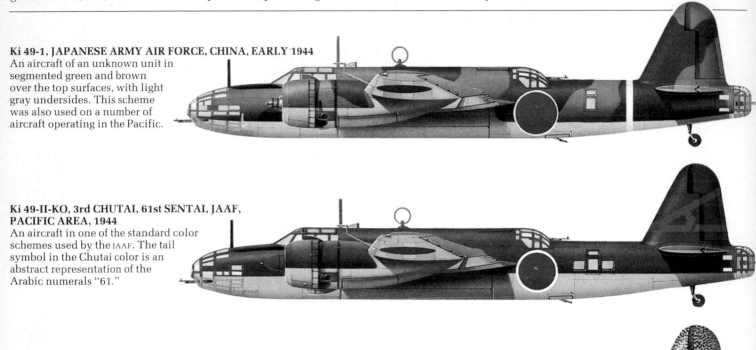

Ki 49-1, JAPANESE ARMY AIR FORCE, CHINA, EARLY 1944
An aircraft of an unknown unit in segmented green and brown over the top surfaces, with light gray undersides. This scheme was also used on a number of aircraft operating in the Pacific.

Ki 49-II-KO, 3rd CHUTAI, 61st SENTAI, JAAF, PACIFIC AREA, 1944
An aircraft in one of the standard color schemes used by the JAAF. The tail symbol in the Chutai color is an abstract representation of the Arabic numerals "61."

Ki 49-II-KO, 1st CHUTAI, 7th SENTAI, JAAF, NEW GUINEA, 1943
A finely executed dark green ribbon camouflage applied over a light gray base color. This scheme is similar to the "wave mirror" finishes sprayed on anti-shipping Ju 88s of the Luftwaffe.

Fighter; the MC 202 'Folgore' (Lightning) was a major advance in fighter performance for the Regia Aeronautica; German DB601 engine gave them a machine capable of outperforming Allied fighters such as the Hurricane; from this was developed the MC 205.

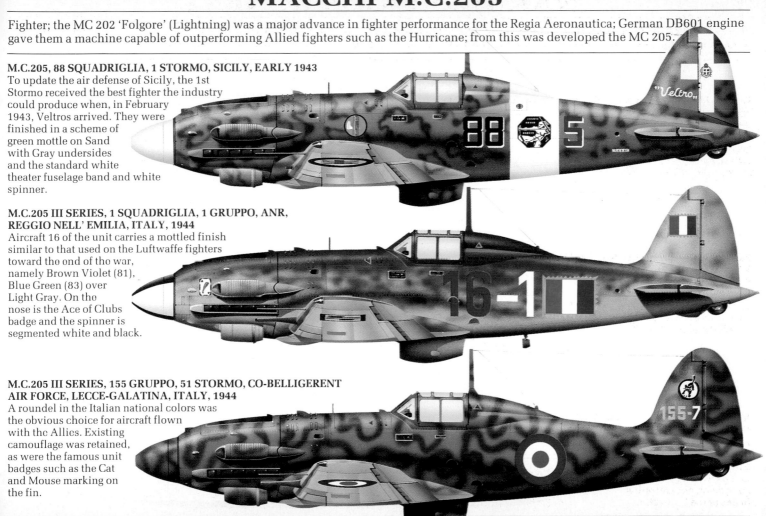

M.C.205, 88 SQUADRIGLIA, 1 STORMO, SICILY, EARLY 1943

To update the air defense of Sicily, the 1st Stormo received the best fighter the industry could produce when, in February 1943, Veltros arrived. They were finished in a scheme of green mottle on Sand with Gray undersides and the standard white theater fuselage band and white spinner.

M.C.205 III SERIES, 1 SQUADRIGLIA, 1 GRUPPO, ANR, REGGIO NELL' EMILIA, ITALY, 1944

Aircraft 16 of the unit carries a mottled finish similar to that used on the Luftwaffe fighters toward the ond of tho war, namely Brown Violet (81), Blue Green (83) over Light Gray. On tho nose is the Ace of Clubs badge and the spinner is segmented white and black.

M.C.205 III SERIES, 155 GRUPPO, 51 STORMO, CO-BELLIGERENT AIR FORCE, LECCE-GALATINA, ITALY, 1944

A roundel in the Italian national colors was the obvious choice for aircraft flown with thc Allies. Existing camouflage was retained, as were the famous unit badges such as the Cat and Mouse marking on the fin.

B-24 LIBERATOR

Bomber; bomb carrying capacity of 8000lb; top speed of 300mph at 30,000ft; 18,482 manufactured across nine major variations; its 2000-mile range made the Liberator much sought after, and the most manufactured American World War II plane.

B-24D, 93rd BOMB GROUP, USAAF, HARDWICK, UK, 1943
Standard Olive Drab and Neutral Gray finish with the short-lived red-outline to the national insignia, individual aircraft letter (N) on the lower fin and group symbol above, overlapping on to the rudder. This was the oldest B-24 Group in the 8th AF and flew more missions than any other unit. After the war the unit flew the B-29, B-47 and, more recently, the B-52.

B-24D-90, 491st BOMB GROUP, USAAF, NORTH PICKENHAM, UK, AUTUMN 1944
To assist the huge 8th AF bomber formations to form up in the right order and position, each group had a brightly-painted lead ship on which the rest of the unit would formate. This done, the lead ship would head for home, leaving the group to the mission. *Little Gramper* is typical and, like most lead ships, was a war-weary aircraft.

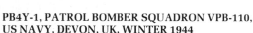

PB4Y-1, PATROL BOMBER SQUADRON VPB-110, US NAVY, DEVON, UK, WINTER 1944
Anti-U-boat patrols over the Atlantic was one of the tasks of these aircraft based in the west of England. Colors were non-specular Sea Blue on the top surfaces, intermediate Blue on the vertical surfaces with Insignia White undersides.

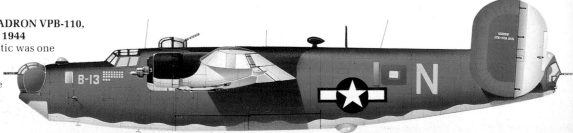

Bomber; first flew in August 1940 and was supplied to USAAF as well as allied air forces; widely known as the 'Mitchell', it was a popular plane with pilots due to its docility; by the war's end nearly 11,000 had been built.

B-25C-10, 487th BOMB SQUADRON, 340th BOMB GROUP, CATANIA, SICILY, SEPTEMBER 1943

Commonly known as "Desert pink," the top surface color applied to the early Mediterranean-based Mitchells was officially called Desert Sand. However, the yellow pigment faded after prolonged exposure to sunlight, resulting in a pronounced pinkish shade. The undersides were Sky Blue. The red-bordered "star and bar" was short-lived – it was initiated in June 1943 and *officially* removed on 14 August 1943, the red being replaced by blue.

Mk II, 320 (NETHERLANDS) SQUADRON, 2 GROUP, RAF DUNSFOLD, UK, APRIL 1944

Very active during the run-up to D-Day In June were the Bomber Command Mitchells of the Dutch units. This Dark Green, Medium Gray example displays six mission symbols on the nose together with a small yellow triangle denoting its crew's nationality.

B-25J-32, 499th BOMB SQUADRON (MEDIUM), 345th BOMB GROUP, USAAF, IE SHIMA, JULY 1945

"Bats Outa Hell" was one of a number of units operating solid-nosed attack B-25s against the Japanese over Kyushu and the Sea of Japan. The eight .50 caliber guns in the nose and the further four on the fuselage sides produced a withering hail of lead.

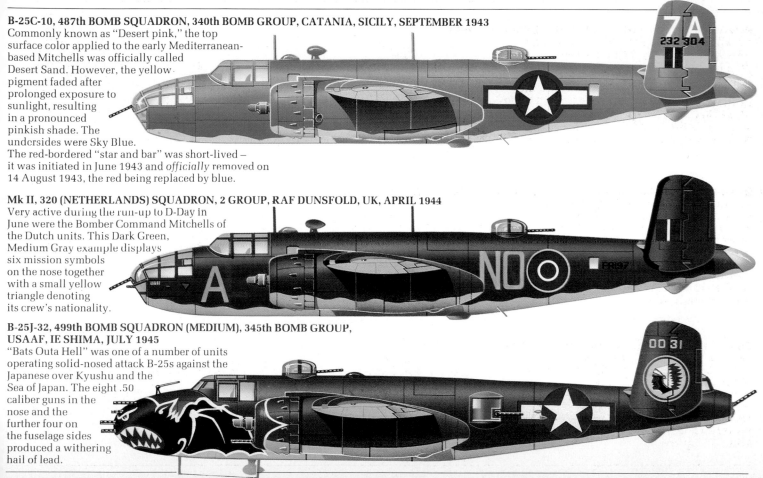

MITSUBISHI G4M 'BETTY'

Bomber; the naval operated 'Betty' had a range of over 3,700 miles achieved by structural lightness and an almost total disregard for armored protection; lack of armor was to prove its great weakness when Allied opposition increased later in the war.

G4M1, 705th KOKUTAI, IMPERIAL JAPANESE NAVY, RABAUL, 1943
Official orders covered the camouflaging of IJN aircraft throughout the Pacific war. This example carries a segment pattern of Dark Green (N2), Medium-Brown (N11) with Light Gray (N10) undersurfaces. The fuselage Hinomaru could be applied on a white square as here or with a 75mm white surround. Unusually this aircraft is devoid of the yellow wing leading edge strip.

G4M1, 761st KOKUTAI, IMPERIAL JAPANESE NAVY, KANOYA, 1943
Apart from the black anti-glare panel in front of the cockpit, this aircraft carries a Dark Green overall finish. The first digit on the fin indicates the basic mission of the aircraft, in this case 3 shows it to be a torpedo bomber. Other included 1=fighter, 2=dive bomber and 4=trainer.

G4M1, TAKAO KOKUTAI, IMPERIAL JAPANESE NAVY, RABAUL, OCTOBER 1942
During the war, a Kokutai equated to a Group formed of three Hikotai each equipped with up to 24 aircraft; the Hikotai was the equivalent of a squadron. This light-colored example is believed to have been in natural metal finish with a dark green mottle over the top surfaces.

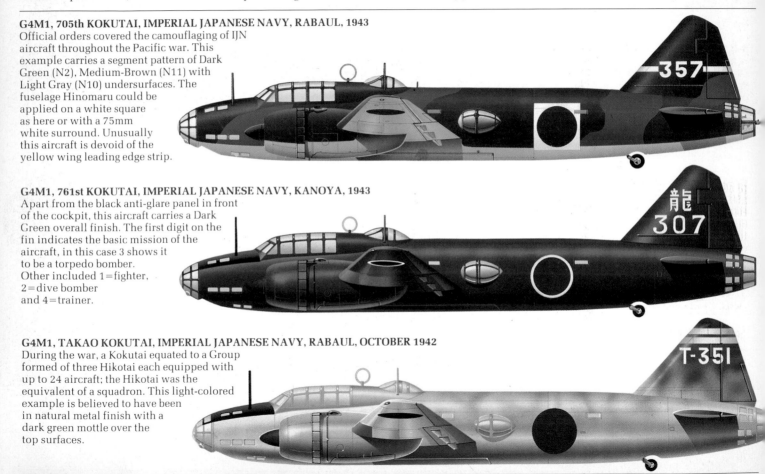

Bomber/reconnaissance; a heavier and more powerful version of the Hudson, the Ventura was known as B-34 in USAAF and PV-1 in US Navy; with the RAF it failed as a daylight bomber over Europe and was withdrawn in mid-1943 after 394 had been delivered.

Mk II, 21 SQUADRON, RAF METHWOLD, UK, MID-1943
Losses forced RAF Bomber Command to withdraw the Ventura after only a year. In service its colors were Dark Green, Dark Earth and Sky with red codes and, on some aircraft, red serials.

PV-1, VB-135, US NAVY, ALEUTIAN ISLANDS, 1944
The official US Navy camouflage for anti-submarine warfare aircraft during this period was Gull Gray Dark (top surfaces), Gull Gray Light (sides) and Non-specular White (undersides). The white serial is painted in an unusually non-standard style.

RB-34, ROYAL NEW ZEALAND AIR FORCE, WHENUAPAI, 1946
New Zealand received 143 Venturas including 23 RB-34 Lexingtons although these were not used on operations. As ex-USAAF machines they were finished in medium green and neutral gray.

FOCKE-WULF Fw 190

Fighter; considered one of the best of World War II; combined large air-cooled radial engine with a tapering fuselage structure; design allowed development of variants for close air support (190F) and fighter-bomber (190G); more than 19,000 had been produced by 1945.

Fw 190A-5, II GRUPPE JAGDGESCHWADER 54, PETSERI, ESTONIA, EARLY 1944

The famous "Grünherz" unit which saw combat throughout the war, carried its insignia on the fuselage of its Bf 109s and, later, the Fw 190s. Yellow Eastern Front markings brightened the dull two-tone green scheme but tended to compromise the overall camouflage effect.

Fw 190A-5/U8, I GRUPPE SCHNELLKAMPFGESCHWADER (SKG) 10, POIX, FRANCE, MID-1943

To cloak their tip-and-run, dawn/dusk, low-level fighter-bomber attacks on UK targets, these Jabo "Butcher Birds" (Luftwaffe slang for the Fw 190) were given a coat of matt black paint over all markings. Only a poorly defined letter revealed the aircraft's identity.

Fw-190A-8, II GRUPPE JAGDGESCHWADER 4, BABENHAUSEN, GERMANY, 1945

During the last months of the war greens and grays were the favored colors. The triple bands are "Defense of the Reich" markings applied for quick identification and were applied to aircraft from 20 February 1945.

GRUMMAN HELLCAT

Carrier-based fighter; the Hellcat finally wrested air superiority from the Zero during the Pacific war; a brutish, inelegant fighter the F6F-3s armament comprised six .50 caliber wing-mounted machine guns; the later F6F-5 had provision for underwing ordnance.

F6F-3, VF-27, US NAVY, USS *PRINCETOWN* (CVL-23), MID-1944
This was the standard counter-shaded Navy scheme comprising semi-gloss Sea Blue on the upper surfaces, matt White undersides to compromise between dark cloudy and bright blue skies when viewed from below, and Intermediate Blue on the sides to blend the top and bottom colors. This finish was retained until March 1944, when Glossy Sea Blue overall was introduced.

F6F-5, VF-12, US NAVY, USS *RANDOLPH* (CV-15), EARLY 1945
With Japan on the retreat across the Pacific, US Navy combat aircraft received this Glossy Sea Blue finish, and a range of markings was introduced to identify the carriers from the aircraft operated. White stripes on Hellcat 65 denoted *Randolph*, and both wing ailerons were also painted white.

HELLCAT Mk 1, 800 SQUADRON, ROYAL NAVY, HMS *EMPEROR*, MEDITERRANEAN, MID-1944
The RN received 252 F6F-3s as Mk 1s and 800 Sqn was the first unit to equip, later taking their aircraft to cover the invasion of the south of France in August 1944. Camouflage under the invasion bands was Dark Slate Gray and Extra Dark Sea Gray with Sky undersides.

DE HAVILLAND MOSQUITO

Fighter/bomber/reconnaissance; constructed of wood and developed initially as a fast, twin-engined, unarmed bomber; two Merlin engines gave the MK IX a top speed of 397mph; fighter had 20mm cannon and four .303 machine guns.

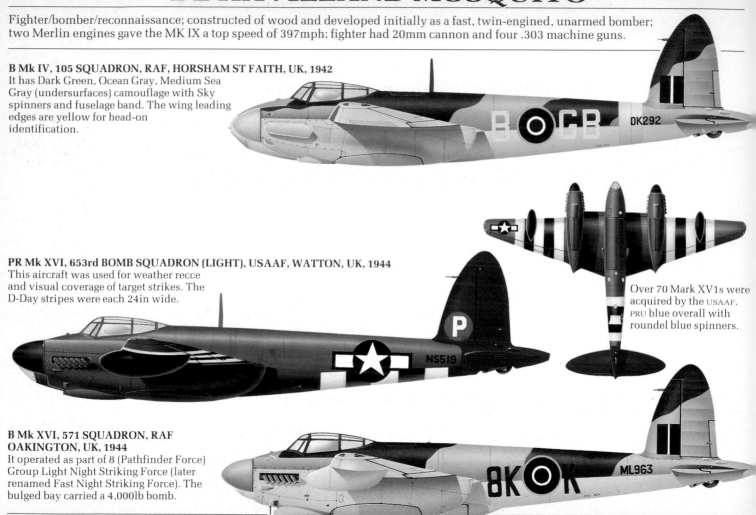

B Mk IV, 105 SQUADRON, RAF, HORSHAM ST FAITH, UK, 1942
It has Dark Green, Ocean Gray, Medium Sea Gray (undersurfaces) camouflage with Sky spinners and fuselage band. The wing leading edges are yellow for head-on identification.

PR Mk XVI, 653rd BOMB SQUADRON (LIGHT), USAAF, WATTON, UK, 1944
This aircraft was used for weather recce and visual coverage of target strikes. The D-Day stripes were each 24in wide.

Over 70 Mark XV1s were acquired by the USAAF. PRU blue overall with roundel blue spinners.

B Mk XVI, 571 SQUADRON, RAF OAKINGTON, UK, 1944
It operated as part of 8 (Pathfinder Force) Group Light Night Striking Force (later renamed Fast Night Striking Force). The bulged bay carried a 4,000lb bomb.

MARTIN B-26 MARAUDER

Bomber; the Marauder was possibly the sleekest bomber of World War II, but it was plagued with problems and the nearly canceled it; powered by two Pratt & Whitney Double Wasp engines; 5157 were built before it was withdrawn USAAF in 1948.

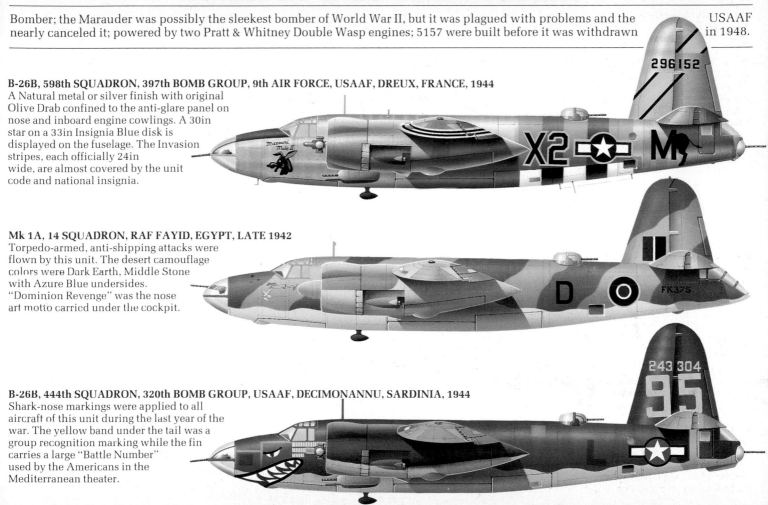

B-26B, 598th SQUADRON, 397th BOMB GROUP, 9th AIR FORCE, USAAF, DREUX, FRANCE, 1944
A Natural metal or silver finish with original Olive Drab confined to the anti-glare panel on nose and inboard engine cowlings. A 30in star on a 33in Insignia Blue disk is displayed on the fuselage. The Invasion stripes, each officially 24in wide, are almost covered by the unit code and national insignia.

Mk 1A, 14 SQUADRON, RAF FAYID, EGYPT, LATE 1942
Torpedo-armed, anti-shipping attacks were flown by this unit. The desert camouflage colors were Dark Earth, Middle Stone with Azure Blue undersides. "Dominion Revenge" was the nose art motto carried under the cockpit.

B-26B, 444th SQUADRON, 320th BOMB GROUP, USAAF, DECIMONANNU, SARDINIA, 1944
Shark-nose markings were applied to all aircraft of this unit during the last year of the war. The yellow band under the tail was a group recognition marking while the fin carries a large "Battle Number" used by the Americans in the Mediterranean theater.

BELL P-39 AIRACOBRA

Fighter; turbo-supercharger engine; armament included a 37mm cannon firing through the propeller hub; 9588 manufactured; the Airacobra was completely outfought by the Zero but was effective in the USSR as a low-level close-support fighter.

AIRACOBRA I, 601 "COUNTY OF LONDON" SQUADRON, RAF DUXFORD, UK, AUGUST 1941

After only a few disappointing months of operations, the RAF withdrew the Airacobra from fighter sweeps over the Continent and sent the remaining aircraft to the USSR. Camouflage was Dark Green and "Mixed Gray," with Medium Sea Gray undersides. In the white of the fin flash is the 601 Sqn sword motif.

P-400, 67th FIGHTER SQUADRON, 347th FIGHTER GROUP, USAAF, NEW GUINEA, 1942

An ex-British ordered example complete with black BW167 serial under the tail and retaining the RAF Dark Green and Dark Earth camouflage. This unit also operated from Guadalcanal, scoring its first victory on 24 August 1942. The red disk in the center of the star was probably removed about this time.

P-39Q, V-VS (SOVIET AIR FORCE), SOUTHERN SECTOR, EASTERN FRONT, USSR, 1944

Aircraft of Russian ace Major Alexander Pokryshkin, who recorded his victories in small red stars on the nose cowling of his aircraft. A total of 55 is shown.

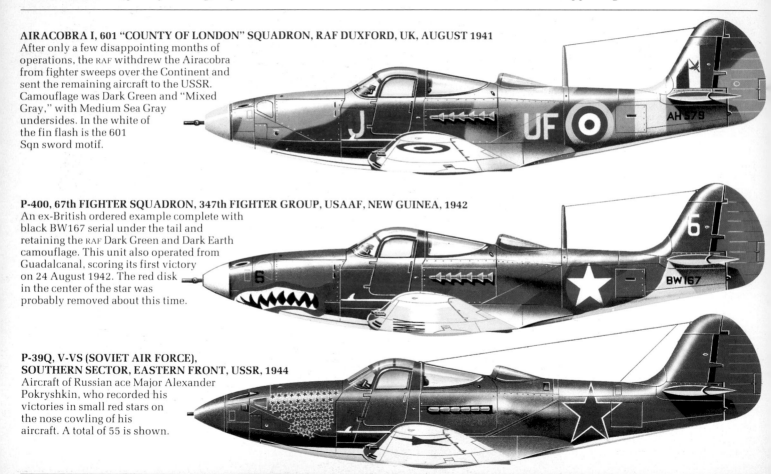

VOUGHT F4U CORSAIR

Fighter-bomber; most important naval fighter-bomber of World War II; early career plagued with problems but came to be known to Japanese as 'Whistling Death'; from May 1940 to January 1953 12581 were built.

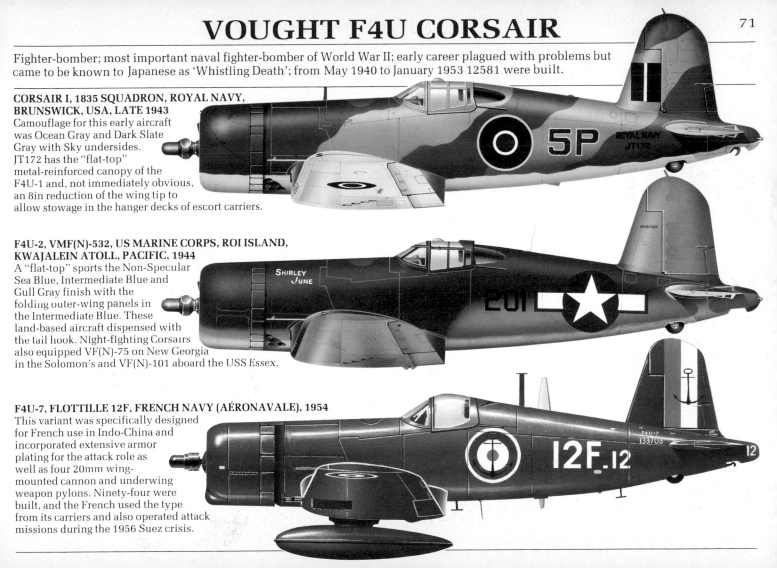

CORSAIR I, 1835 SQUADRON, ROYAL NAVY, BRUNSWICK, USA, LATE 1943

Camouflage for this early aircraft was Ocean Gray and Dark Slate Gray with Sky undersides. JT172 has the "flat-top" metal-reinforced canopy of the F4U-1 and, not immediately obvious, an 8in reduction of the wing tip to allow stowage in the hanger decks of escort carriers.

F4U-2, VMF(N)-532, US MARINE CORPS, ROI ISLAND, KWAJALEIN ATOLL, PACIFIC, 1944

A "flat-top" sports the Non-Specular Sea Blue, Intermediate Blue and Gull Gray finish with the folding outer-wing panels in the Intermediate Blue. These land-based aircraft dispensed with the tail hook. Night-fighting Corsairs also equipped VF(N)-75 on New Georgia in the Solomon's and VF(N)-101 aboard the USS *Essex*.

F4U-7, FLOTTILLE 12F, FRENCH NAVY (AÉRONAVALE), 1954

This variant was specifically designed for French use in Indo-China and incorporated extensive armor plating for the attack role as well as four 20mm wing-mounted cannon and underwing weapon pylons. Ninety-four were built, and the French used the type from its carriers and also operated attack missions during the 1956 Suez crisis.

PETLYAKOV PE-2

Light bomber, trainer and reconnaissance; 11,427 manufactured; the Pe-2 was prominent in repelling the German invasion of the USSR; most widely used was the -2FT which incorporated modifications demanded by the front-line crews.

Pe-2FT, 34 GUARDS BOMBER AVIATION REGIMENT, POLAND, AUGUST 1945
Many wartime aircraft, and not only Russian, were paid for by members of the civilian population. This aircraft was donated by the people of Leningrad, the inscription reads "Leningrad-Königsberg."

Pe-2FT, 3 DIVE BOMBER REGIMENT, 1st POLISH COMPOSITE AIR CORPS, 1945
This was one of the three P3-2 equipped units operational in the summer of 1945. Naturally, red was a favored color, in most forms of insignia among Eastern Bloc air forces.

Pe-2, 46 BOMBER, AVIATION REGIMENT, MOSCOW MILITARY DISTRICT, USSR, WINTER 1941
Like the Germans, the Soviet AF did its best to conceal its dark-painted aircraft once the snows came. A liberal coating of white paint was applied over all top surfaces, but the effect of airflow and general operational wear and tear soon wore down the covering to give this unkempt appearance.

Pe-2FT, 73rd BOMBER AVIATION REGIMENT, RED BANNER BALTIC FLEET, 1942
This aircraft has a distinctly worn appearance, indicative of the intensive operations flown by these light bombers at this stage of the war. It was operating in the Leningrad area at the time.

Fighter; overweight despite its wooden construction, the aircraft had just entered production when Germany invaded the USSR in 1941; at one stage 12 Lagg-3s were being completed daily and 6528 had been built when production ceased in autumn 1942.

LaGG-3, V-VS (RED BANNER BALTIC FLEET AIR FORCE), FINLAND, MARCH 1942

Finished in a disruptive scheme of green and brown paint, this example was shot down over Finland and found to have a thick layer of polish to smooth the exterior surfaces. Three examples were later operated by the Finnish Air Force as high-speed reconnaissance aircraft.

LaGG-3, 178th REGIMENT, 6 FIGHTER AIR CORPS, MOSCOW, USSR, 1942–3

The Soviet Air Force had its share of aces, such as Captain (later Colonel) Gerasim Grigoryev, deputy CO of the unit. His white-distempered winter-finish aircraft shows 15 victory stars on the rear fuselage.

LaGG-3, 9th REGIMENT, BLACK SEA FLEET AIR FORCE, MAY 1944

An intricate lion's head artwork on a red heart was an unusual embellishment for aircraft that were almost constantly on operations, but Yuri Shchipov or his groundcrew obviously found the time to apply it. Eight victory stars are under the cockpit sill.

LOCKHEED P-38 LIGHTNING

Twin-engined-interceptor; twin-boom layout with central nacelle for the pilot, a battery of guns, a tricycle undercarriage and turbochargers for the engines; early problems were resolved and it served with distinction on every US war front.

P-38F-5, 347th FIGHTER GROUP, 13th AIR FORCE, USAAF, GUADALCANAL, SOLOMON ISLANDS, 1943
The F was the first fully operational version to enter service and when flown at its rated altitude it could defeat most single seat fighters. Shark-mouth markings on this Olive Drab/Neutral Gray aircraft brighten up an otherwise standard color scheme for the period.

P-38J, 338th FIGHTER SQUADRON, 55th FIGHTER GROUP, 8th AIR FORCE, NUTHAMPSTEAD, UK, SPRING 1944
Standard ETO scheme on an aircraft used for fighter escort duties during the American daylight bomber offensive over Europe. A point of interest is that this unit had apparently ignored the USAAF order that yellow and white checkerboard markings were to be applied to spinners and engine cowlings from March 1944.

P-38J, 401st FIGHTER SQUADRON, 370th FIGHTER GROUP, FLORENNES, BELGIUM, NOVEMBER 1944
Part of the 9th Air Force, this group carried geometric symbols on the outer surfaces of its aircrafts' tails – triangle for 401st, circle for 402nd and square for 485th – with the aircraft letter painted on the inside surface (in this case "N"). The unit coverted to P-51s in 1945.

Fighter; the Mustang was a triumph of design simplicity taking only 117 days for the prototype to be produced; 800 Mustang 1s with Allison engines were delivered to the RAF before the Rolls-Royce Merlin was adopted and the aircraft found its true worth.

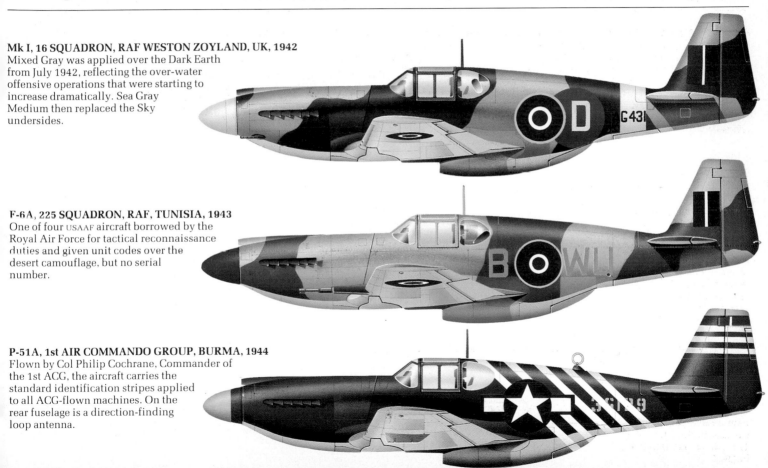

Mk I, 16 SQUADRON, RAF WESTON ZOYLAND, UK, 1942
Mixed Gray was applied over the Dark Earth from July 1942, reflecting the over-water offensive operations that were starting to increase dramatically. Sea Gray Medium then replaced the Sky undersides.

F-6A, 225 SQUADRON, RAF, TUNISIA, 1943
One of four USAAF aircraft borrowed by the Royal Air Force for tactical reconnaissance duties and given unit codes over the desert camouflage, but no serial number.

P-51A, 1st AIR COMMANDO GROUP, BURMA, 1944
Flown by Col Philip Cochrane, Commander of the 1st ACG, the aircraft carries the standard identification stripes applied to all ACG-flown machines. On the rear fuselage is a direction-finding loop antenna.

AVRO LANCASTER

Heavy bomber; developed from the Avro Manchester, it was the most successful heavy bomber of World War II; with four Merlin engines it could lift bomb loads of up to 22,000lbs; production totalled 7,374 and it continued in RAF service until 1956.

PROTOTYPE LANCASTER, AEROPLANE AND ARMAMENT EXPERIMENTAL ESTABLISHMENT, UK, 1941
This aircraft, which first flew on 9 January 1941, has a Type A1 fuselage roundel, a black serial and yellow undersurfaces denoting its non-operational function.

"PICCADILLY PRINCESS," B Mk I, 424 (TIGER) SQUADRON, ROYAL CANADIAN AIR FORCE, SKIPTON-ON-SWALE, UK, 1945
It has, rather unusually, light blue codes with the Type C1 roundel. Nose art was a particular feature of Canadian-operated aircraft.

B Mk III, 617 SQUADRON, RAF CONINGSBY, UK, 1943
This aircraft is specially modified for the attack of the Mohner, Eder and Sorpe Dams. It has the standard Dark Red codes and serial (note G=Guard suffix). The mid-upper turret has been deleted and the bomb-bay cut away.

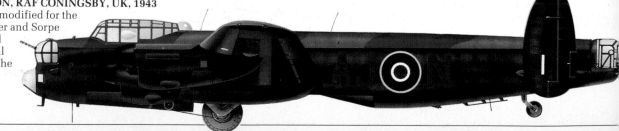

B Mk VI, 635 SQUADRON, RAF, DOWNHAM MARKET, UK, 1944
This late Lancaster version had increased performance for Pathfinder duties and carried radar jamming devices. Note the absense of nose and mid-upper turrets.

B Mk I (SPECIAL), 617 SQUADRON, RAF WOODHALL SPA, UK, 1945
Shown here camouflaged for daylight operations with Type C roundels above and below the wings. It is shown carrying a "Grand Slam" bomb.

B Mk VIII, 9 SQUADRON, RAF, INDIA, 1946
White upper surfaces were ordered in February 1945 for "Tiger Force" aircraft destined for the war against Japan. The surrender took place before the aircraft began operations.

ILYUSHIN Il-2

Ground-attack fighter-bomber; built in greater numbers than any other combat aircraft, it was the outstanding ground-attack machine of World War II; carrying 1300lb of bombs and rockets, it could survive considerable damage; production reached nearly 38,000.

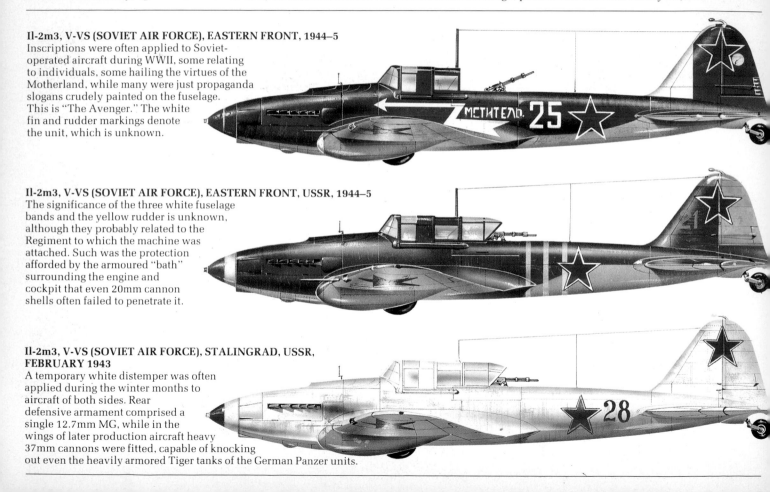

Il-2m3, V-VS (SOVIET AIR FORCE), EASTERN FRONT, 1944–5
Inscriptions were often applied to Soviet-operated aircraft during WWII, some relating to individuals, some hailing the virtues of the Motherland, while many were just propaganda slogans crudely painted on the fuselage. This is "The Avenger." The white fin and rudder markings denote the unit, which is unknown.

Il-2m3, V-VS (SOVIET AIR FORCE), EASTERN FRONT, USSR, 1944–5
The significance of the three white fuselage bands and the yellow rudder is unknown, although they probably related to the Regiment to which the machine was attached. Such was the protection afforded by the armoured "bath" surrounding the engine and cockpit that even 20mm cannon shells often failed to penetrate it.

Il-2m3, V-VS (SOVIET AIR FORCE), STALINGRAD, USSR, FEBRUARY 1943
A temporary white distemper was often applied during the winter months to aircraft of both sides. Rear defensive armament comprised a single 12.7mm MG, while in the wings of later production aircraft heavy 37mm cannons were fitted, capable of knocking out even the heavily armored Tiger tanks of the German Panzer units.

NORTH AMERICAN HARVARD

Trainer; by far the most important training aircraft of World War II; more than 20,000 manufactured in US and under license abroad; called BC-1, AT-6, and T-6 Texan in US service, whilst in Britain and Commonwealth countries it was called the Harvard.

Mk 1, No 2 FLYING TRAINING SCHOOL, ROYAL AIR FORCE, 1939–40
The standard trainer scheme used from 1938 through the opening stages of World War II. Markings include the 2 FTS badge below the cockpit and the gas patch applied over the rear fuselage (designed to change color should the aircraft fly through a gas cloud).

Mk II, No. 2 WIRELESS SCHOOL, ROYAL CANADIAN AIR FORCE, 1942
The serial number indicates that this aircraft was originally destined for the RAF, but was diverted to Canada for training use.

AT-6A, ROYAL SWEDISH AIR FORCE, EARLY 1950s
Sweden bought a number of surplus ex-USAAF Texans after WWII, giving them the designation Sk 14A. These remained in service until the early 1970s. Dayglo patches ensured a higher degree of visibility for training use.

REPUBLIC P-47

Fighter; a large and rather ugly aircraft compared with the Spitfire, the Thunderbolt soon proved itself in combat; from its first flight in May 1941 to final delivery in September 1945 some 15,660 were built.

P-47D-20-RA, 19th FIGHTER SQUADRON, 318th FIGHTER GROUP, USAAF, SAIPAN, MARIANAS, JULY 1944
The personal aircraft of Maj Henry McAfee, "Miss Mary Lou" carries four victory marks in the form of Japanese flags under the cockpit. The unit had natural metal cowlings and tails to distinguish its aircraft, the white letter C being the identity letter of this particular machine.

P-47D-25-RE, 352nd FIGHTER SQUADRON, 353rd FIGHTER GROUP, USAAF, RAYDON, UK, JULY 1944
To answer complaints of a lack of rearward vision, a bubble canopy was fitted to aircraft from the D-25 series. "Butch II" has invasion bands and a disruptive camouflage of Dark Green and Ocean Gray with natural metal undersides. Serial number was 42-26459.

P-47D-25-RE, 1 GRUPO DE CACA, BRAZILIAN AIR FORCE, TARQUINIA, ITALY, NOVEMBER 1944
This unit formed the fourth squadron attached to the 350th FG, the last of the 12th AF "Jug" (short for Juggernaut) units to form in the Mediterranean theater. Manned by Brazilians, it used Olive Drab/ Neutral Gray-finished aircraft with the national star marking applied over the US version, unit badge and 30in high recognition code on the engine cowling.

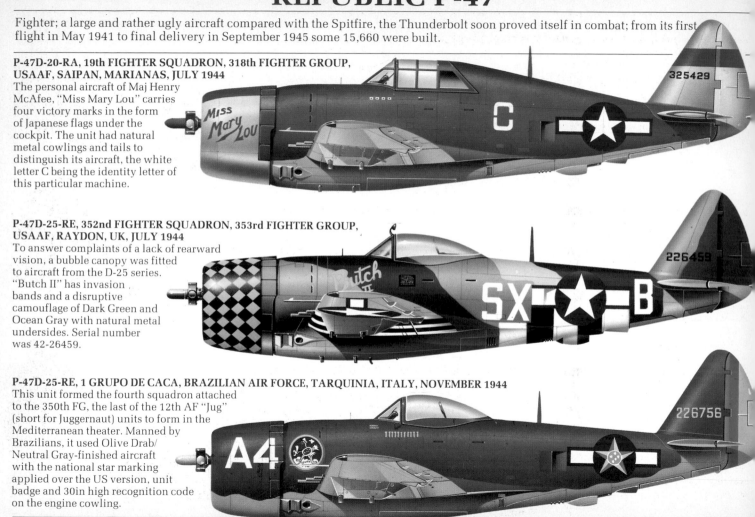

P-47D-30-RA, 366th FIGHTER SQUADRON, 358th FIGHTER GROUP, USAAF, TOUL, FRANCE, 1944
Shown following its transfer to the 1st
Tactical Air Force, this aircraft has the
letter/number code (1A), the 1st TAF 18in red
cowl and the orange tail unit. The
dorsal fin fillet (introduced on the
D-40 version and retrofitted)
reduced a tail flutter problem
associated with the loss of the
original "razorback" fuselage.

P-47D, 86th FIGHTER SQUADRON, 79th FIGHTER GROUP, USAAF, FANO, ITALY, FEBRUARY 1945
Receiving its first P-47s in March 1944, this
unit adopted the coding system used
previously on its P-40s. Sometimes as a
prefix, as here, or as a suffix, the
letter X and a number provided
quick identification of the
unit in the air, enhanced by
the lightning insignia on the tail and
the red base to the engine cowling.
The anti-glare panel fore and aft of
the canopy was in Olive Drab.

P-47M-1, 63rd FIGHTER SQUADRON, 56th FIGHTER GROUP, USAAF, BOXTED, UK, SPRING 1945
The fastest production "Jug" of all was the M
with a top speed of 473mph at 32,000ft. The
56th was the last P-47-equipped unit in the 8th
AF and received Ms in early 1945.
Colors used by the 63rd FS were dark
and light blue shadow shading
with natural metal undersides
and code letters. A medium blue
was used for the serial number and
rudder.

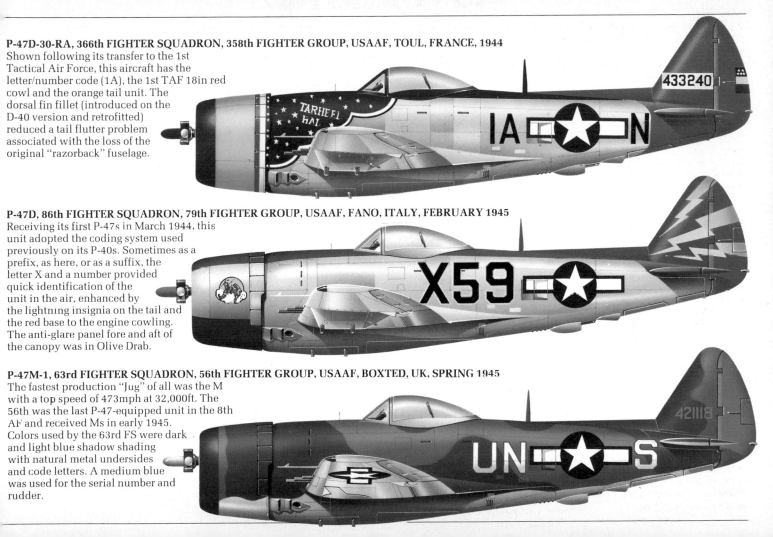

DOUGLAS A-26 INVADER

Bomber; entered service in the last year of World War II; it was found to be fast and capable of carrying twice the specified bomb load and a range of gun armaments could be fitted to produce a formidable ground attack aircraft.

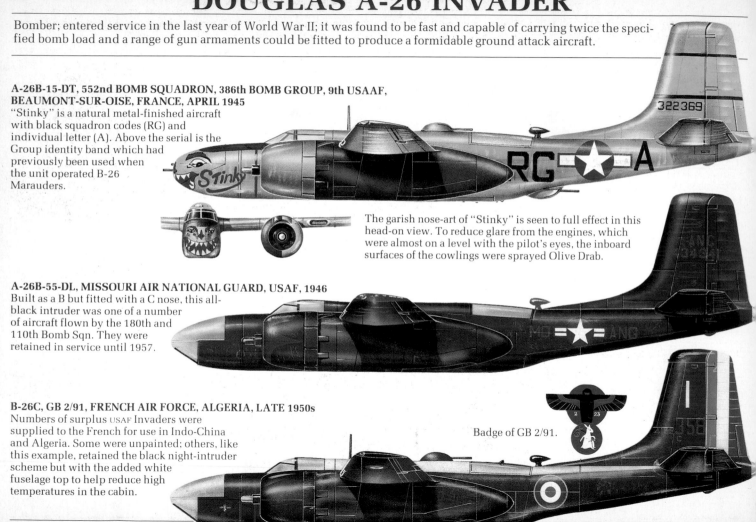

A-26B-15-DT, 552nd BOMB SQUADRON, 386th BOMB GROUP, 9th USAAF, BEAUMONT-SUR-OISE, FRANCE, APRIL 1945

"Stinky" is a natural metal-finished aircraft with black squadron codes (RG) and individual letter (A). Above the serial is the Group identity band which had previously been used when the unit operated B-26 Marauders.

The garish nose-art of "Stinky" is seen to full effect in this head-on view. To reduce glare from the engines, which were almost on a level with the pilot's eyes, the inboard surfaces of the cowlings were sprayed Olive Drab.

A-26B-55-DL, MISSOURI AIR NATIONAL GUARD, USAF, 1946

Built as a B but fitted with a C nose, this all-black intruder was one of a number of aircraft flown by the 180th and 110th Bomb Sqn. They were retained in service until 1957.

B-26C, GB 2/91, FRENCH AIR FORCE, ALGERIA, LATE 1950s

Numbers of surplus USAF Invaders were supplied to the French for use in Indo-China and Algeria. Some were unpainted; others, like this example, retained the black night-intruder scheme but with the added white fuselage top to help reduce high temperatures in the cabin.

Badge of GB 2/91.

BLACKBURN FIREBRAND

Torpedo bomber; spent most of the 1939-45 war on trials and only reached squadrons in 1945; intended to have the Sabre engine but these were all allocated to the Hawker Typhoon and so the Centaurus was used; 225 aircraft of all marks were built.

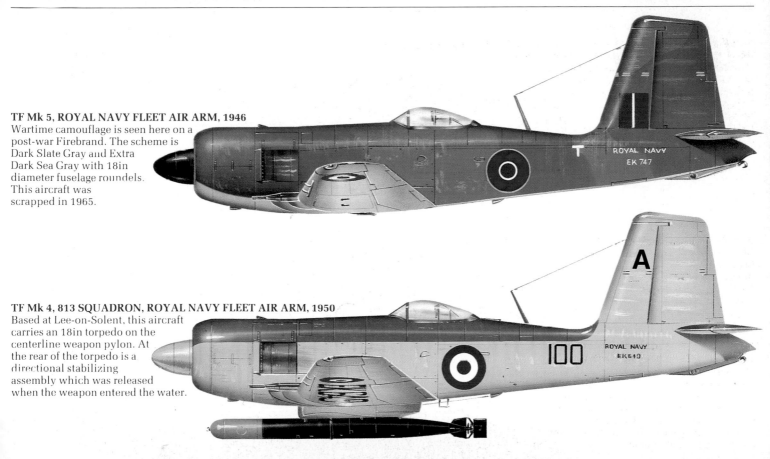

TF Mk 5, ROYAL NAVY FLEET AIR ARM, 1946
Wartime camouflage is seen here on a post-war Firebrand. The scheme is Dark Slate Gray and Extra Dark Sea Gray with 18in diameter fuselage roundels. This aircraft was scrapped in 1965.

TF Mk 4, 813 SQUADRON, ROYAL NAVY FLEET AIR ARM, 1950
Based at Lee-on-Solent, this aircraft carries an 18in torpedo on the centerline weapon pylon. At the rear of the torpedo is a directional stabilizing assembly which was released when the weapon entered the water.

BOEING B-29 SUPER-FORTRESS

Heavy bomber; first flew in September 1942 and became USAAF's major weapon against Japan's war industry; bomb load 10 tons and defensive armament in remote-controled positions totaled 10 .50in MGs and one 20mm cannon; dropped atomic bombs on Japan.

B-29-1-BW, 468th BOMB GROUP, 58th BOMB WING (VERY HEAVY), USAAF, INDIA, NOVEMBER 1944

Only very early aircraft were delivered in Olive Drab/Neutral Gray camouflage, this machine being the 29th production Superfortress. Stripped of arnament it was used to transport fuel from India to China – hence the name "Esso Express" and the 30 camel-shaped mission symbols on the nose.

B-29-45-BW, 500th BOMB GROUP, 73rd BOMB WING, USAAF, PACIFIC, 1945

"Z" on the tail indicates the group, the black bar on the dorsal fin is a "lead crew" flash and the green fuselage band is believed to be a squadron indicator.

RB-29A-45-BN, 91st STRATEGIC RECONNAISSANCE SQUADRON, OKINAWA, JAPAN, 1953

A reconnaissance Superfortress flew the last B-29 mission of the Korean War on 27 July 1953. Over the three years only 16 B-29s were lost to North Korean fighters, four to AA fire and 14 to other operational causes: not bad for a 10-year-old bomber up against jet-powered MiGs.

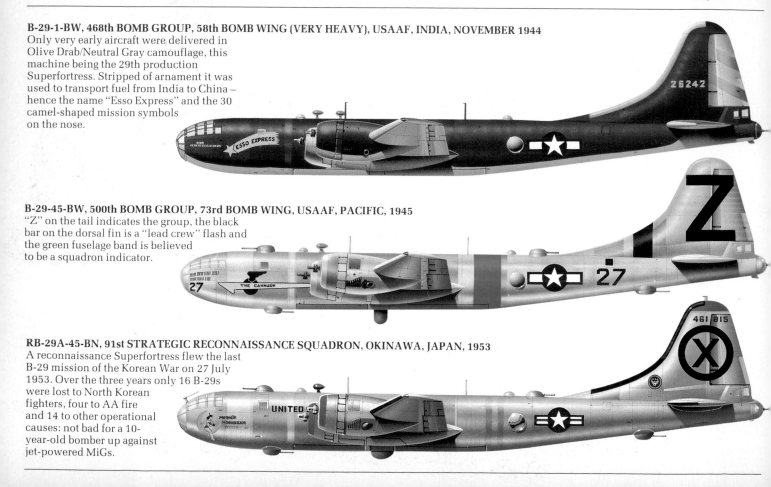

LOCKHEED NEPTUNE

Maritime patrol and reconnaissance; prototype first flew in May 1945; seven major variants with production reaching 1051; late production aircraft had their piston engines supplemented by underwing jet pods; a refined turboprop version is still operational.

MR Mk 1, 217 SQUADRON, RAF KINLOSS, UK, 1954
One of 52 P2V-5 Neptunes supplied to the UK and operated by Coastal Command between 1952 and 1957. The US Glossy Sea Blue finish was retained. The single letter A is the unit code.

AP-2H, VAH-21, US NAVY, CAM RANH BAY, SOUTH VIETNAM, 1968
Four of these highly modified aircraft were used to monitor sections of the Ho Chi Minh Trail using electronic sensors. The color scheme is a matt Dark Gull Gray. Light Gull Gray and Mixed Gray (50–50 Light and Dark Gull Gray).

SP-2H, 10 SQUADRON, ROYAL AUSTRALIAN AIR FORCE, TOWNSVILLE, AUSTRALIA, 1975
This was the last Neptune version built and Australia received 12 for patrol duties along the country's eastern seaboard before they were replaced by Electras from 1977.

LOCKHEED P-80

Fighter-bomber; the first practical jet combat aircraft accepted into USAAF service; prototype flew on 8 January 1944 powered by a British de Havilland H1 turbo-jet; it saw action in Korea where it operated with considerable success; production totaled 1718.

P-80A, 412th FIGHTER GROUP, 1946
Immediate post-war period finish of glossy light gray overall. Believed to be the squadron commander's aircraft due to the multi-colored fuselage bands. The red had yet to reappear in the national insignia.

F80B, 94th FIGHTER SQUADRON, LADD FIELD, ALASKA, 1947
Famous as the "Hat-in-a-Ring" unit. The aircraft carries a "Buzz" number prefixed P signifying Pursuit, changed in June 1948 to F for Fighter.

F-80C, 36th FIGHTER-BOMBER SQUADRON, 8th FIGHTER-BOMBER WING, KOREA, 1949
This aircraft carries a typical Korean War scheme of a polished natural metal with an Olive Drab anti-glare panel in front of cockpit. This aircraft is believed to have carried the name "Miss Barbara Ann" on the other side of the nose.

Fighter/fighter-bomber; developed during World War II, eventually entered service with the Royal Navy as the Sea Fury; acquitted itself well in Korea even against North Korean MiG-15 jets; the Fury was exported to a number of countries and production totaled 864.

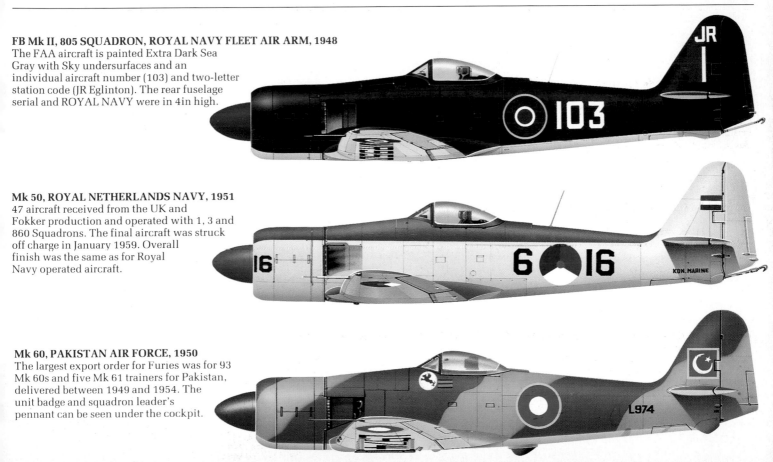

FB Mk II, 805 SQUADRON, ROYAL NAVY FLEET AIR ARM, 1948
The FAA aircraft is painted Extra Dark Sea Gray with Sky undersurfaces and an individual aircraft number (103) and two-letter station code (JR Eglinton). The rear fuselage serial and ROYAL NAVY were in 4in high.

Mk 50, ROYAL NETHERLANDS NAVY, 1951
47 aircraft received from the UK and Fokker production and operated with 1, 3 and 860 Squadrons. The final aircraft was struck off charge in January 1959. Overall finish was the same as for Royal Navy operated aircraft.

Mk 60, PAKISTAN AIR FORCE, 1950
The largest export order for Furies was for 93 Mk 60s and five Mk 61 trainers for Pakistan, delivered between 1949 and 1954. The unit badge and squadron leader's pennant can be seen under the cockpit.

A.W. METEOR

Day and night fighter; single-seat and two seat versions; for night fighter armament was moved to the wings and radar was housed in the nose along with a second seat for the operator; first flight was December 1948 and final production totaled 547.

NF. Mk 11, 68 SQUADRON, RAF WAHN, WEST GERMANY, 1952
This aircraft carries the commanding officer's stripes on the fin and the station commander's pennant on the nose.

NF. Mk 13, EGYPTIAN AIR FORCE, 1955
This aircraft was the second of six refurbished ex-RAF planes sold to Egypt which retained their original camouflage whilst in EAF service.

TT. Mk 20, ROYAL NAVY FLEET REQUIREMENTS UNIT, HAL FAR, MALTA, EARLY 1960s
This carries base codes on the fin and a serial number (WD 785) under the tailplane. There is a wind-driven target sleeve winch above the starboard wing.

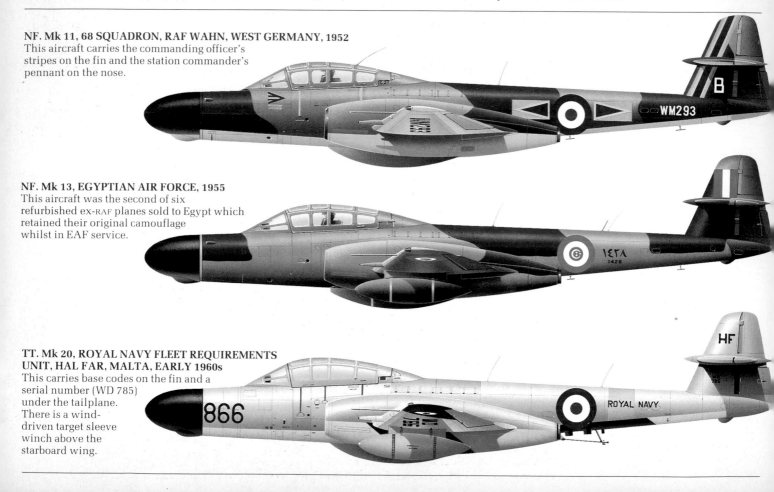

DOUGLAS AD-1 SKYRAIDER

Fighter-bomber; this was the largest single seat production aircraft when it entered service in 1947; capable of a 10 hour flight endurance; seven weapons pylons under each wing; called the AD-1 and later the A-1, it was an extremely robust machine.

A-1H (AD-6), VA-145 "SWORDSMEN," US NAVY, NAS ATSUGI, JAPAN, EARLY 1960s
Gloss Gull Gray and White aircraft with the unit badge on a green band, aircraft serial number beneath the code and the individual number (04) repeated on the fin tip. During the Korean War this unit was designated Attack Squadron 702, flying early AD-1s; it became VA-145 in late 1952 and took later "Spads" to Vietnam in 1964.

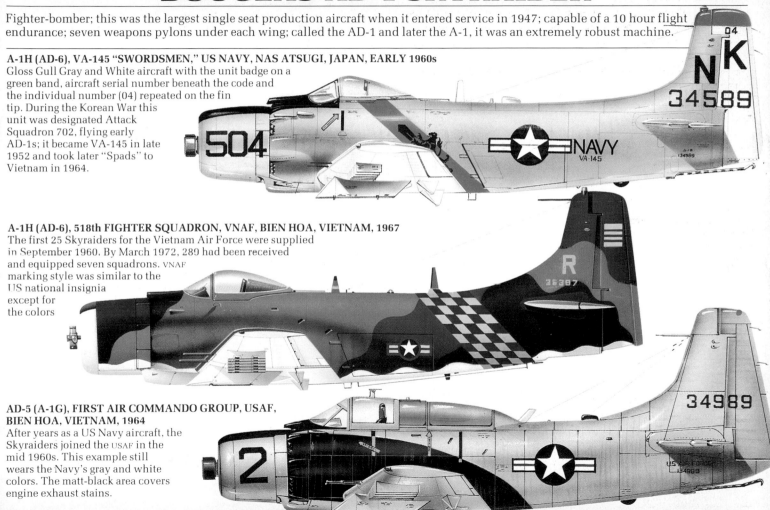

A-1H (AD-6), 518th FIGHTER SQUADRON, VNAF, BIEN HOA, VIETNAM, 1967
The first 25 Skyraiders for the Vietnam Air Force were supplied in September 1960. By March 1972, 289 had been received and equipped seven squadrons. VNAF marking style was similar to the US national insignia except for the colors

AD-5 (A-1G), FIRST AIR COMMANDO GROUP, USAF, BIEN HOA, VIETNAM, 1964
After years as a US Navy aircraft, the Skyraiders joined the USAF in the mid 1960s. This example still wears the Navy's gray and white colors. The matt-black area covers engine exhaust stains.

DE HAVILLAND VAMPIRE

Fighter-bomber; single seater entered RAF service in 1946 too late to see service in World War II; tapering wings and tail supported on slim booms gave it an unmistakable shape; RAF had 40 squadrons and the aircraft was widely exported, total production reaching 4206.

FB. Mk 5, 112 SQUADRON, RAF BRUGGEN, WEST GERMANY, 1953
It has Dark Green, Dark Sea Gray and PR Blue undersides. There is an 18in diameter roundel on the boom.

FB. Mk 5, FRENCH AIR FORCE, 1950
Known as the Mistral to the French Air Force, 247 were built under license in France.

FB. Mk 5, 2 SQUADRON, RHODESIAN AIR FORCE, THORNHILL, RHODESIA, 1971
It has dark green and brown upper surface camouflage with a national markings adopted on declaration of UDI in 1970.

FB. Mk 6, SWISS AIR FORCE, MID-1950s
This was the fifth Swiss Vampire built under license out of 100 produced by F+W, Emmem, from 1951. The finish is silver overall.

NORTH AMERICAN F-86 SABRE

Fighter; the dominant jet in Korea where its qualities overcame Chinese MiG-15s, it was the successful outcome of US engineering genius combined with German wartime research on swept wings; prototype flew in 1947; eventual production totaled 9502.

F Mk 4, 92 SQUADRON, RAF FIGHTER COMMAND, LINTON-ON-OUSE, UK, 1954
US Mutual Aid funds were used to provide 430 Canadair-built Sabres to the RAF in the mid-1950s. Finish was Dark Green, Dark Sea Gray and Light Gray undersides. On the nose is a small squadron badge.

Mk 6, JG 71 "RICHTHOFEN," WEST GERMAN AIR FORCE, WITTMUNDHAFEN, 1963
Three Luftwaffe day fighter Wings operated 225 of the Canadair-built Sabre's. The bright unit markings on JG 71 aircraft are a variation of a scheme carried on the unit's Messerschmitt 109s during WWII. The Richthofen association goes back to World War I.

F-86F, 2 SQUADRON, SOUTH AFRICAN AIR FORCE, KOREA, 1953
Between March and October 1952, the SAAF's "Flying Cheetah" squadron operated 20 or so Sabres in the natural metal scheme over Korea. The broad yellow band was an identification marking and the over-large fin stripes were also applied to assist with visual recognition.

CONVAIR B-36

Heavy bomber; originally intended to attack German targets from the USA, the first flight did not take place until August 1946; this ten-engined bomber was dogged with severe technical problems and it was withdrawn from service in 1959.

B-36A, 7th BOMB GROUP (HEAVY), 8th AIR FORCE, SAC, USAF, CARSWELL, USA, EARLY 1950s

This aircraft, one of a number of A versions, was nothing more threatening than a crew trainer, although it was later converted into an RB-36E. The aircraft lacks the later underwing jet pods, relying on the six Pratt & Whitney Wasp Majors to drive the 19ft diameter propellers.

B-36B-1-CF, STRATEGIC AIR COMMAND, USAF, EARLY 1950s

This was the eighth of 73 B models built and carries a large "Buzz" number on the fuselage for identification purposes. Arctic markings were applied to many aircraft during this period, when the Cold War appeared likely to erupt into a full-scale conflict requiring "over the Pole" operations.

RB-36E, 72nd STRATEGIC RECONNAISSANCE SQUADRON, 5th SR WING, SAC, USAF, TRAVIS AFB, USA, 1951–8

Very few B-36s were painted, most retaining their natural metal finish. This example was built as a bomber, but converted to carry a 14-camera installation in the forward bomb-bay. It bears the X in-a-circle marking of the 15th Air Force.

B-36H, 11th BOMB WING, STRATEGIC AIR COMMAND, USAF, CARSWELL, USA, MID-1950s

The U in-a-triangle identifies the Bomb Wing which flew this version of the B-36. On the fin is the famous 'Winged 8' of the 8th Air Force.

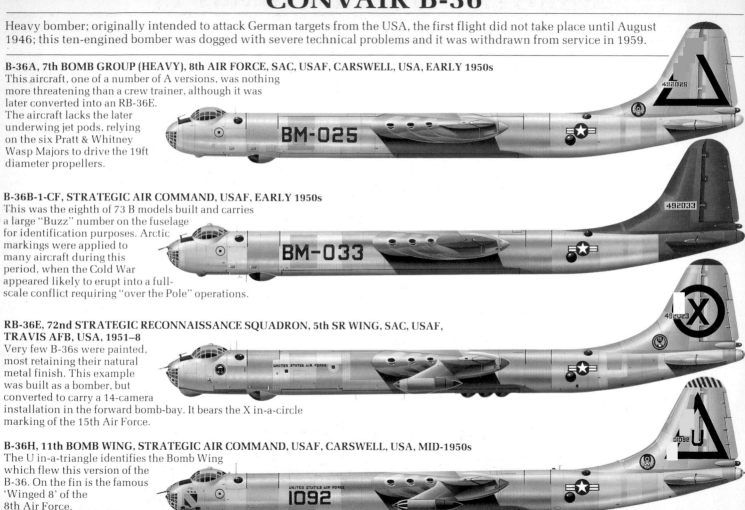

MIKOYAN-GUREVICH MiG-15

Fighter; based on captured German swept wing research; early models were equipped with the British Nene jet engine; actually entered service before the US F-86 Sabre; the superiority achieved by the Sabre in Korea was probably due to superior pilot training.

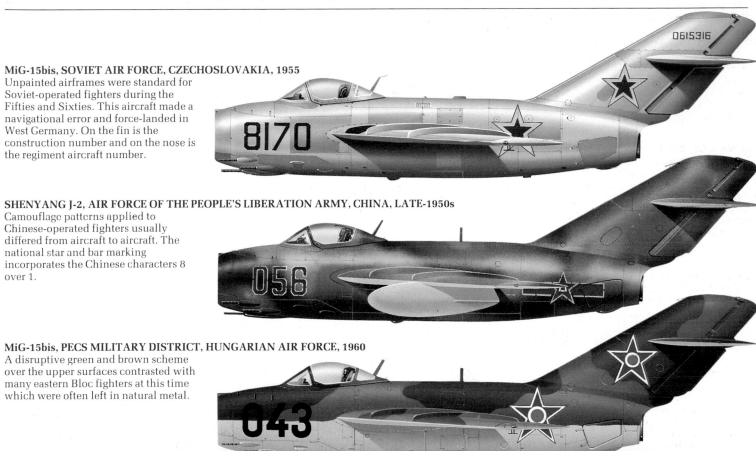

MiG-15bis, SOVIET AIR FORCE, CZECHOSLOVAKIA, 1955
Unpainted airframes were standard for Soviet-operated fighters during the Fifties and Sixties. This aircraft made a navigational error and force-landed in West Germany. On the fin is the construction number and on the nose is the regiment aircraft number.

SHENYANG J-2, AIR FORCE OF THE PEOPLE'S LIBERATION ARMY, CHINA, LATE-1950s
Camouflage patterns applied to Chinese-operated fighters usually differed from aircraft to aircraft. The national star and bar marking incorporates the Chinese characters 8 over 1.

MiG-15bis, PECS MILITARY DISTRICT, HUNGARIAN AIR FORCE, 1960
A disruptive green and brown scheme over the upper surfaces contrasted with many eastern Bloc fighters at this time which were often left in natural metal.

GRUMMAN PANTHER/COUGAR

Carrier-based fighter/bomber; the US Navy's first jet-powered carrier based fighter-bomber to see action when it attacked targets in Korea; initial straight-winged Panther series gave way to the swept-wing F9F-6 Cougar; total produced of both variants was 3367.

F9F-2, VF-781, US NAVY, KOREA, 1951-2
A Panther in typical glossy, but worn Sea Blue finish of the Korean War period. Squadron markings were usually painted on the tip tanks as well as the nose area and the top of the fin. On many missions the Panthers, having unloaded their underwing ordnance, assumed a fighter role, using their four 20mm cannon to good effect against the poorly flown MiGs and Yaks.

F9F-5P, VMJ-3, US MARINE CORPS, KOREA, 1953
'Midnight Blue' unarmed photo-reconnaissance Panther with camera bay in the nose; 36 were built. The 'Marines' title on the rear fuselage had been introduced in February 1950 after a lapse of nine years; the letters were 12in high.

F9F-8, VF-61, US NAVY, MID-1950s
A Cougar of 'The Jolly Rogers' (today VF-84), identified by the swept wing with no tip tank and the undernose blister for the UHF antenna. The dark coloring was to last until July 1955, when the Light Gull Gray and White was adopted, becoming Fleet-wide by mid-1957.

Utility helicopter; first major load-carrying helicopter with acceptable performance; prototype first flew in November 1949; powered by a radial engine in the nose, driving a three-bladed rotor and a small anti-torque tail rotor; 1281 were produced.

HO4S-3, UNITED STATES NAVY, EARLY 1950s

The Navy first ordered the S-55 as the HO4S-1 in April 1950, first deliveries being made at the end of the year for general purpose and anti-submarine observation. The -3 had a higher-powered 700hp Wright R-1300 engine. The type was redesignated UH-19F in 1962.

H-19C, US ARMY, MID-1950s

Starting in 1952, the US Army received 2 C and 336 D versions for utility and assault duties. The Red Indian name 'Chickasaw' was given to the type, and the designation changed in 1962 to UH-19C and D series. Olive Drab was the overall color.

BOEING B-47

Medium bomber; Boeing incorporated swept wings into this its first multi-engined turbojet bomber; prototype first flew in 1947 but development was slow and first production models appeared in 1952; over 1800 eventually equipped 81 squadrons.

B-47E-46-BW, USAF STRATEGIC AIR COMMAND, LATE 1950s

Like the RAF's V-bombers, SAC B-47s were given an anti-radiation gloss white finish over the undersides to reduce the effects of a nuclear flash. The top surfaces were left aluminum with a matt black surround to the two-seat cockpit. The Command sash and badge was applied to the port side of the nose, the Wing badge to the starboard side.

B-47E-130-BW, 307th BOMB WING, USAF, LINCOLN AFB, USA, LATE 1950s

This late-production aircraft, one of 1359 Es built at Wichita, has large 1780 US gal drop-tanks between the engines. Each aircraft could carry up to 20,000lb of bombs internally; defensive armament was limited to two 20mm cannon in the tail turret.

RB-47H, 343rd STRATEGIC RECONNAISSANCE SQUADRON, 55th SRW, USAF, 1957

Signals intelligence (SIGINT) was the role of these so-called "spy-planes." Despite the 24in high title on the nose and the 50in-diameter star on the side of the fuselage, at least one was shot down by Soviet fighters. Covered in aerials and strange pods, these aircraft carried three "crows" (systems operators) in a bomb-bay compartment.

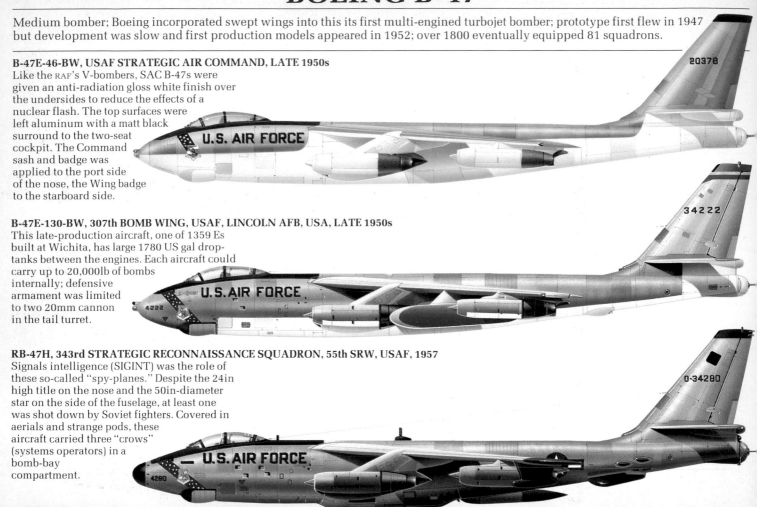

Heavy bomber; entered service in 1955 and still operational in 1992; used in the Gulf War where missions were undertaken from US and UK bases; crew of six; eight turbojet/turbofan engines; can be used for air launching cruise missiles or the sea-skimming Harpoon.

B-52D, 367th BOMB SQUADRON, 306th BOMB WING, McCOY AFB, USA, 1971
The tall pointed tail identified the early variants. It was the D version, painted in the scheme shown here, that pounded North Vietnam. The SE Asia colors were Tan (34201), Green (34079), Green (34159) and Black (17038). The nose markings include a SAC badge and the legend "ORLANDO . . . where the action is." On the fin is the symbol of the 2nd Air Force.

B-52G, STRATEGIC AIR COMMAND, US AIR FORCE, 1980
Devoid of any markings other than the standard serial in black on the fin tip (repeated on the nose) and the national insignia, which is hidden by the wing in this view, on the fuselage side, this G variant has the latest electro-optical viewing system blisters under the nose. White undersides replaced the black of the Vietnam era.

B-52G, STRATEGIC AIR COMMAND, US AIR FORCE, 1988
The latest color combination consists of two dark grays and a green which SAC chose in 1985 to conceal B-52s better in their low-level attack role. The result is a particularly somber finish; but it is non-reflective, which reduces its visibility when viewed from above against the ground.

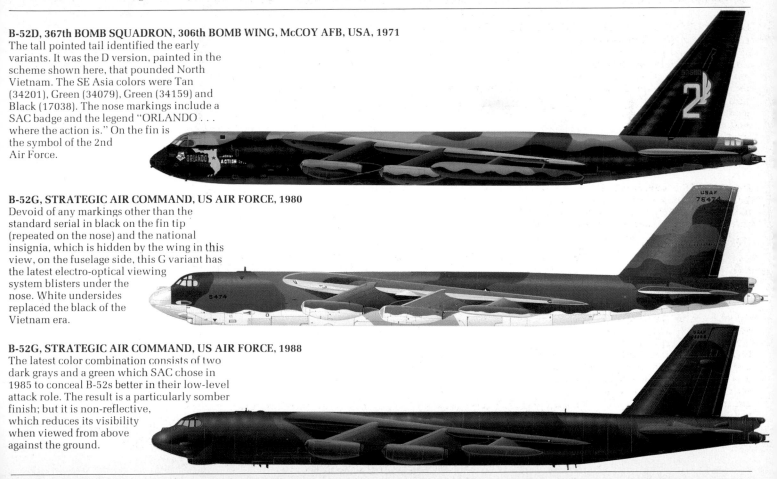

McDONNELL DOUGLAS A-4

Fighter-bomber; designed for US Navy carrier use, the 'Skyhawk' first went to sea in 1954 and is still operational in various countries; small wing for carrier stowage; carried enough fuel to give respectable combat range; 2960 produced.

A-4C, VA-144, USS KITTYHAWK, US NAVY, EARLY 1960s
Light Gull Gray and Gloss White undersides and markings that typify the early Sixties. The Carrier Air Wing code is on the fin; the aircraft number is displayed on the nose and the last four digits of the serial are enlarged on the dorsal fin.

A-4M, VMA-324, US MARINE CORPS, BEAUFORT, S CAROLINA, 1972
This was the first Marine unit to fly the A-4M. VMA-324 displayed its badge on the intake sides. Improved pilot visibility was a major feature of this version which had a redesigned canopy and more ammunition for the wing-root 20mm guns.

OA-4M, H&MS-32, US MARINE CORPS, CHERRY POINT, USA, 1986
Shown here in current low-visibility two-tone gray colors (Compass Gray and Light Compass Gray) with outline insignia countershaded on the fuselage. By now even the bright rescue markings have been toned down.

A-4Q, 3 ESCUADRILLA AERONAVAL DE ATAQUE, 3 ESCUADRA, ARGENTINE NAVY, RIO GRANDE, ARGENTINA, 1982
Here is the Dark Green and White camouflage used at the time of the Falklands conflict. The unit code on the fuselage combines the individual aircraft number (04). 0657 on fin is manufacturer's construction number.

A-4KU, KUWAIT AIR FORCE, AL JAHRA, KUWAIT, 1982
A standard Middle Eastern desert finish of Brown, Sand and Deep Sky Blue was applied to 30 single-seat Skyhawks equipping two units of the Kuwait Air Force. The Arabic script reads 514.

A-4E, 11 SQUADRON, INDONESIAN ARMED FORCES/AIR FORCE, MADIUN, INDONESIA, 1987
An unusual three-color scheme applied to an ex-Israeli A-4E bought in 1980. 12 Sqn at Pekanbaru is another operator of the type. Note the extended jetpipe to reduce the effect of a hit by heat-seeking missiles.

REPUBLIC F-84

Fighter-bomber; the F-84 started life as a straight-wing jet-powered aircraft but was outclassed by MiG-15s in Korea; the swept-wing version, F-84F, became NATO's main nuclear weapons carrier from 1954; 3428 manufactured.

F-84F, 315 SQUADRON, ROYAL NETHERLANDS AIR FORCE, EINDHOVEN, NETHERLANDS, 1968

Six squadrons of F-84Fs and one squadron of RF-84Fs totaling 204 aircraft operated in the RNethAF from the mid-1950s. The red outlined areas on the fuselage are inspection panels, whilst the two parallel red lines under the rear fuselage are trestle points used for maintenance purposes.

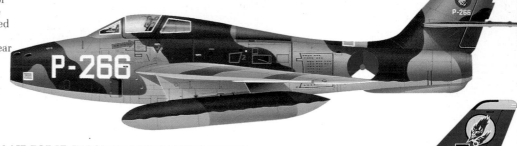

RF-84F, 1 STAFFEL AG 51, WEST GERMAN AIR FORCE, INGOLDSTADT-MANCHING, 1960

The Luftwaffe had two Wings of RF-84Fs, each with two 26-aircraft squadrons, equipped between July 1959 and January 1967. The unit's devil's head emblem shown on the fin of this red-tailed aircraft gave way shortly afterwards to an owl which currently adorns AG 51s RF-4E Phantoms.

RF-84F, 1 ESC. "BELFORT," 33 ESC. DE RECONNAISSANCE, FRENCH AIR FORCE, LUXEUIL, FRANCE, 1966

Disruptive green-gray camouflage covers the top surfaces of this aircraft with the unit's battle axe emblem by the engine intake and the unit number and aircraft code flanking one of the oblique camera ports.

HAWKER HUNTER

Fighter; Rolls Royce Avon engine; four 30mm Aden cannons, plus bombs, rockets and/or drop tanks; the good-looking and highly successful Hunter served in 21 air arms and was once the backbone of RAF Fighter Command; a total of 1,972 were produced.

F. Mk 6, 43 SQUADRON, RAF LEUCHARS, UK, LATE 1950s
An aircraft of the famous "Fighting Cocks" squadron, camouflaged in gloss Dark Green and Dark Sea Gray with aluminum (silver) undersides.

FR. Mk 71A, FUERZA AEREA DE CHILE, EARLY 1980s
The converted, ex-RAF F.4 (XF317) retains UK day fighter finish, but with Light Aircraft Gray undersides.

T.Mk 75A, 141 SQUADRON, REPUBLIC OF SINGAPORE AIR FORCE, TENGAH, SINGAPORE, EARLY 1980s
This is a trainer version displaying bright markings before high visibility colors were deleted.

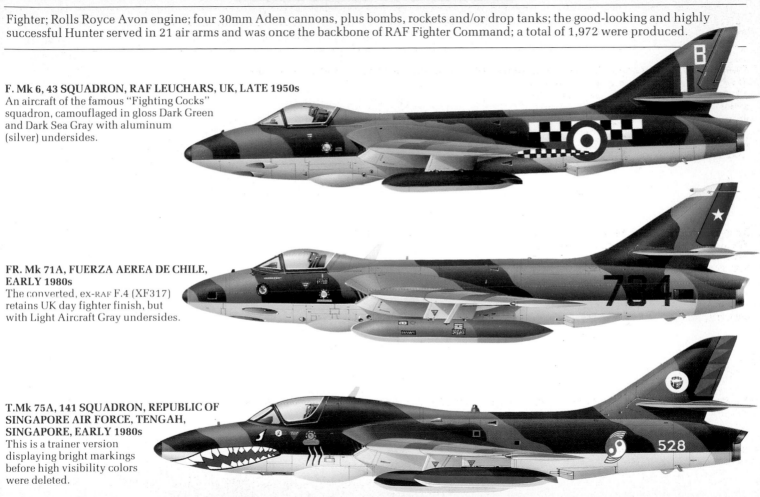

NORTH AMERICAN F-100

Fighter; the first Western fighter capable of level supersonic performance and also the first Century-series fighter in the USAF; other users included Denmark, France and Turkey; variants were the F-100C, D and two-seat F; production totaled 2294.

F-100D, 20th TACTICAL FIGHTER WING, USAF, WETHERSFIELD, UK, 1960

The silver-finished "Huns" of the three squadrons that formed this unit were familiar to residents of East Anglia from the end of the Fifties. At the tip of the fin is the unit badge and alongside is a unit citation award.

F-100F, TACTICAL AIR COMMAND, USAF, 1965

First of a small batch of special Wild Weasel I SAM (Surface-to-Air Missile) suppression conversions operated on Iron Hand flights over North Vietnam in 1965–66. One of the external differences between this aircraft and the trainer version included an additional antenna on the fin.

F-100D, ROYAL DANISH AIR FORCE, DENMARK, 1976

Three squadrons operated F-100s, 725 at Karup and 727 and 730 at Skrydstrup. Aircraft were initially delivered and flown in natural metal finish, but in 1969 low visibility colors were adopted. This particular aircraft crashed in May 1977.

GRUMMAN TRACKER

Anti Submarine aircraft; the Tracker was the first design specifically intended to perform all phases of the ASW mission-detection, identification, tracking and destruction; prototype first flew in December 1954; still in service entering the 1990s.

S-2E, VS-21, US NAVY, USS *KEARSAGE* (CVSG-53), 1964
Lumps and bumps abounded on a 'Stoof' (nickname for the Tracker). Above the cockpit was an ECM antenna, under the fuselage was a retractable radar scanner and under the rudder was a retractable MAD (Magnetic Anomaly Detector) boom; numerous aerials and underwing weapons were also fitted.

S-2E, ESCUADRON ANTISUBMARINO 12, PERUVIAN NAVY, JORGE CHAVEZ AB, LIMA, PERU, 1987
Seven E and four G versions were in recent service with the Peruvian Navy in the scheme shown here. They have been supplied since 1976 and include some of the latest equipment modifications to enable them to conduct ASW missions effectively against modern quiet-running submarines.

S-2E/F, REPUBLIC OF CHINA NAVY, TAIWAN, 1986
This unusual camouflage for over-water use appears to have shades reminiscent of those used by the US Navy in 1943. Colors are similar to Blue Gray, Semi-gloss Sea Blue and Intermediate Blue with what seems like light gray undersides. About 32 of these aircraft are in use.

LOCKHEED C-130 HERCULES

Transport/tanker/gunship/surveillance/ASW/reconnaissance; first flight 23 August 1954 and still in production 37 years later; also a series of civil cargo-carrying Hercules, some with lengthened fuselages adopted by military users.

C-130H, MILITARY AIRLIFT COMMAND, USAF, 1987

For the low-level tactical airlift role, a so-called "Lizard" scheme of Dark Green, Medium Green and Gray was adopted in the early Eighties. The matt black national insignia on the rear fuselage sides is almost invisible.

C Mk 3, TRANSPORT WING, RAF LYNEHAM, UK 1980

First of 30 "stretched" Hercules for the RAF was this aircraft serial no. XV223, converted by Lockheed-Georgia in 1979. Subsequent conversions were done by Marshall of Cambridge.

EC-130Q, VQ-3 & VQ-4, US NAVY, PATUXENT RIVER NAS, USA, 1976

Light Gull Gray and Gloss White colors are displayed on this TACAMO ("Take Charge And Move Out") version specially adapted to communicate with USN missile submarines far from base. 18 have been built so far.

REPUBLIC F-105

Attack bomber; the largest single-seat single-engined combat aircraft in history; designed to deliver nuclear or conventional weapons in all weapons at high speed and long range; bore a major share of the bombing missions in Vietnam.

F-105D, 563rd TFS, 23rd TFW, USAF, VIETNAM, JUNE 1965
Early operations in SE Asia found aircraft such as this example still flying in natural metal finish. On the fin is the Tactical Air Command badge with the serial number below and the last three digits forming the buzz number on the nose.

F-105D, 149th TFS, VIRGINIA AIR NATIONAL GUARD, RICHMOND AFB, USA, LATE 1970s
The single-seater "Thud" was withdrawn from Vietnam bombing operations in 1970 and on return to the USA most of the survivors were spread among ANG units. Personal insignia was usually applied under the wing on the light gray fuselage side as with "Satanic duo" seen here.

F-105G, 561st TFS, 23rd TFW, McConnell AFB, USA, EARLY 1970s
With a Shrike anti radar missile visible on the outboard wing pylon, this "Thud" is in Wild Weasel III configuration for defense suppression operations over Vietnam. The fin code letters are 24in high with 15in high serial numbers. 20mm Vulcan cannon is in nose.

MIKOYAN-GUREVICH MiG-21

Fighter interceptor and fighter-bomber; the delta-winged 'Fishbed' MiGs were the most widely used combat aircraft in the world during the 1970s being operated in at least 38 countries; MiG 21PFMA is the fighter-bomber version; over 10,000 of all versions produced.

MiG-21MF (FISHBED J), SOVIET AIR FORCE, BAGRAM, AFGHANISTAN, 1983
Detached to the occupying Soviet Forces, this aircraft carries a color scheme associated with the southern area of the USSR. The centerline GSh-23L cannon can just be seen behind the 108 Imp gal (490lit) drop tank on the inboard pylon.

MiG-21M, 37 SQUADRON "PANTHERS," INDIAN AIR FORCE, 1981
Externally similar to the MF model, the Hindustan-built M version differed from retaining the earlier Tumanskii R-11 engine. On the nose is the unit badge while the two red triangles by the cockpit indicate both canopy and ejection seat can be fired in an emergency.

MiG-21MF, IRAQI AIR FORCE, 1985
Another desert operator of the Fishbed, Iraq used the type to fly patrols over sensitive military bases which could attract the attention of the Iranian AF, with whom Iraq was at war. The latest MiG-29 Fulcrum is now in service with the Iraqi AF.

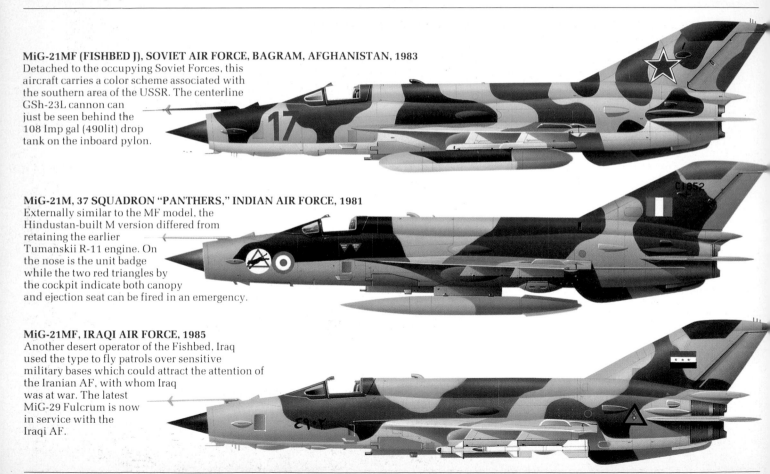

High-altitude reconnaissance; designed and built under a cloak of secrecy with the codename of Aquatone, its true purpose was only revealed when one was shot down over the Soviet Union in 1960; production was approximately 113 aircraft.

U-2A, 4080th STRATEGIC RECONNAISSANCE WING, USAF, LAUGHLIN AFB, USA, 1962
Depicted here in a natural metal overall finish is an aircraft used during the 1962 Cuban missile crisis and later deployed to RAF Upper Heyford, UK. The national insignia was painted above port and below starboard wings only.

U-2CT, 100th STRATEGIC RECONNAISSANCE WING, DAVIS-MONTHAN AFB, USA, 1975
Built initially as a U 2D and operated by the 4080th SRW, 56-6953 was later converted into this trainer configuration and used by the 100th and 9th SRWS.

U-2C, 4080th STRATEGIC RECON. WING, RAF MILDENHALL, UK, 1975
One of six deployed to Europe to test a target location system developed to find Warsaw Pact emitters behind the Iron Curtain. The two-tone gray "Sabre Scheme" replaced black at request of the UK Government.

U-2D, 651st TEST GROUP, USAF AIR RESEARCH AND DEVELOPMENT COMMAND, EDWARDS AFB, USA, JULY 1971
Built as a U-2A, this machine was used to test new equipment following its change to U-2D standard. Painted in non-reflective black, it has an unusual vertical sensor behind the cockpit.

CONVAIR F-102

Fighter interceptor; the 'Deuce' almost failed to reach production being unable to attain Mach-1 in level flight. Aero-dynamic reshaping (the 'Coke-bottle curve') successfully reduced the drag; entered service in April 1956 and production totaled 889.

F-102A, 57th FIGHTER INTERCEPTOR SQUADRON, US AIR FORCE, KEFLAVIK, ICELAND, MID-1960s

The "Black Knights" in Iceland was the last unit to fly this Century-series fighter, finally retiring it in 1973. Red Arctic markings were applied to the fin and wings, a 30in star marking was painted on the engine intake, the "U.S. AIR FORCE" was 21in high, and fin serial numbers were 12in high.

F-102A, 342 MIRA, 114 WING, HELLENIC AIR FORCE, TANAGRA, GREECE, 1974

Vietnam camouflage appeared on some of the 24 or so aircraft supplied to Greece in 1970 (a number of two-seaters were included for training use). However, most had a pale gray finish and were retained in use until replaced by Mirage F.1CGs.

F-102A, 181 SQUADRON, TURKISH AIR FORCE, MERZIFON, TURKEY, 1969–70

About 50 surplus Daggers were supplied to two squadrons of the Turkish AF. Like the Greek machines, they retained the general gray finish and the black serial number on the fin. They are believed to have been used during the Turkish invasion of Cyprus in 1974.

Strategic bomber; maneuverability was almost unequaled by any other large, four-jet strategic bomber; prototype flew in 1952 and withdrawn from service in 1984 after its use in the bombing of the Argentine-held Falklands two years previously.

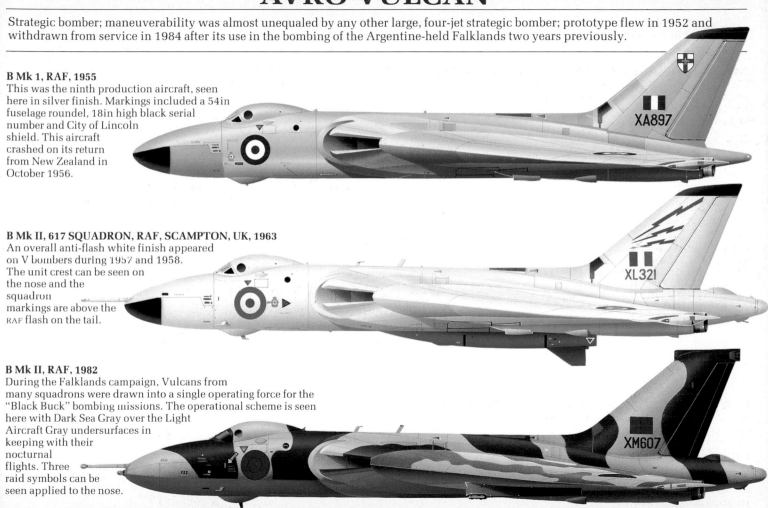

B Mk 1, RAF, 1955
This was the ninth production aircraft, seen here in silver finish. Markings included a 54in fuselage roundel, 18in high black serial number and City of Lincoln shield. This aircraft crashed on its return from New Zealand in October 1956.

B Mk II, 617 SQUADRON, RAF, SCAMPTON, UK, 1963
An overall anti-flash white finish appeared on V bombers during 1957 and 1958. The unit crest can be seen on the nose and the squadron markings are above the RAF flash on the tail.

B Mk II, RAF, 1982
During the Falklands campaign, Vulcans from many squadrons were drawn into a single operating force for the "Black Buck" bombing missions. The operational scheme is seen here with Dark Sea Gray over the Light Aircraft Gray undersurfaces in keeping with their nocturnal flights. Three raid symbols can be seen applied to the nose.

McDONNELL F-101 VOODOO

Fighter/fighter-bomber/reconnaissance; entered service 1957; F101C fighter-bomber and unarmed reconnaissance models served with distinction in Vietnam until supplanted by the Phantom; production exceeded 730 aircraft.

F-101B, 179th FIGHTER INTERCEPTOR SQUADRON, MINNESOTA, AIR NATIONAL GUARD, USA, 1974
A protective light gray paint was sprayed over the natural metal to reduce the effect of corrosion. This F-101B displays its ANG operator insignia and has the Command badge on the fin.

CF-101B, 409 SQUADRON, CANADIAN ARMED FORCES, COMOX, CANADA, 1975
This Air Defense Group aircraft is sprayed overall a light gray. It was one of 56 CF-101Bs and 10, 101Fs delivered to Canada under the Peace Wings operation in 1971, replacing an earlier batch of the same quantity.

RF-101C, 45th TACTICAL RECON. SQUADRON, 460th TRW, USAF, TAN SON NHUT, SOUTH VIETNAM, 1968
Standard SE Asia camouflage of Dark Green, Medium Green and Tan with Gray undersides. The White tail code is 24in high and serial number 15in high, both in stencil style lettering.

CHANCE-VOUGHT F-8 CRUSADER

Carrier-borne fighter; the Crusader was built with a variable-incidence high wing to give greater lift while landing and taking off; it was the first shipboard service fighter to fly at Mach 1 in level flight; total of 1261 built.

F-8A, VF-211 "CHECKMATES," US NAVY, NAS MOFFETT FIELD, USA, EARLY-1960s
Light Gull Gray and Gloss White was the basic color scheme for US-based carrier aircraft for many years. Bright markings such as these were typical of squadron aircraft. On this machine the NP tail code denotes attachment to Carrier Air Group 21.

F-8D, VMF(AW)-451, US MARINE CORPS, USA, MID-1960s
Four Sidewinder AAMs could be carried by this version, of which 152 were built. The squadron code is carried on the fin and below it is a larger than standard serial number. Before designations were changed in the Sixties this version was known as an F8U-2N.

RF-8G, VFP-306, US NAVY RESERVE, NARTU, WASHINGTON DC, USA
This smart example is a remanufactured RF-8A with a camera bay in the forward fuselage. The RF-8 Crusader was the primary naval reconnaissance aircraft throughout the Vietnam War.

HUGHES 500

Light observation helicopter; the egg-shaped OH-6 won a design competition and was given the Indian name 'Cayuse', though troops called it 'Loach' in Vietnam; minigun armed, later variants were the 500 MD with TOW-missiles and nose-mounted sight.

OH-6A, US ARMY, DA NANG, VIETNAM, 1971
Olive Drab, broken only be the black Army titling on the boom, was the overall color for OH-6s. A six barrel GE Minigun is mounted on the port side of the fuselage.

500M, DANISH ARMY FLYING SERVICE, VANDEL, DENMARK, 1980
One of 15 machines delivered in 1971 for observation duties with the Danish Army. In wartime, these would be deployed with units in the field.

500D, FINNISH AIR FORCE, UTTI, FINLAND, 1983
One of two machines (the other being HH-5) that were bought to replace two 500Cs operated in the liaison role. Note the unit badge on the rear door.

ENGLISH ELECTRIC LIGHTNING

Fighter interceptor; the only all-British production fighter capable of flying at Mach 2 or twice the speed of sound; maiden flight in August 1954; entered RAF service in 1960; eight basic marks and production totaled 337.

F Mk 3, 56 SQUADRON, RAF WATTISHAM, UK, 1965
This was the heyday of bright markings for the RAF which were to last for about a year. The colors were gloss on the natural metal (silver) finish. The "Phoenix-arising" emblem was positioned on the nose flash of 56 Squadron Lightnings at this time and some emblems appeared on a white background.

F Mk 6 11 SQUADRON, RAF BINBROOK, UK, 1984
This aircraft has toned down markings on Medium Sea Gray with Barley Gray undersides – all semi-matt.

F Mk 2A, 92 SQUADRON, RAF GÜTERSLOH, WEST GERMANY, 1975
For low level intercept duties, Dark Green was applied over top surfaces but natural metal still remained underneath.

CONVAIR F-106

Fighter interceptor; derived from the F102B and improved to such an extent that another number was allocated; underwent various improvement programs and 340 aircraft were produced in total but they were never to be proven in combat.

F-106A, 460th FIGHTER INTERCEPTOR SQUADRON, USAF, OXNARD AFB, USA, 1968
One of 13 squadrons of Air Defense Command to have operated Darts, the 460th displays colorful insignia associated with this defender of the USA. Around the fuselage are the squadron commander's stripes.

F-106A, 159th FIS, 125th FIGHTER INTERCEPTOR GROUP, FLORIDA ANG, JACKSONVILLE, USA, 1975
This unit was one of several Air National Guard formations to get F-106s in the early 1970s. Super Falcon missiles or Genie rockets were the type's main armament, and some were fitted with an underbelly gun pack with a 20mm cannon.

F-106B, 195th FIS, CALIFORNIA AIR NATIONAL GUARD, FRESNO, USA, 1980
The longer canopy and raised fuselage top-line of the two-seat conversion trainer is shown to advantage in a side view. The cut-out in the middle of the fuselage is for the tanker probe for air-to-air refueling.

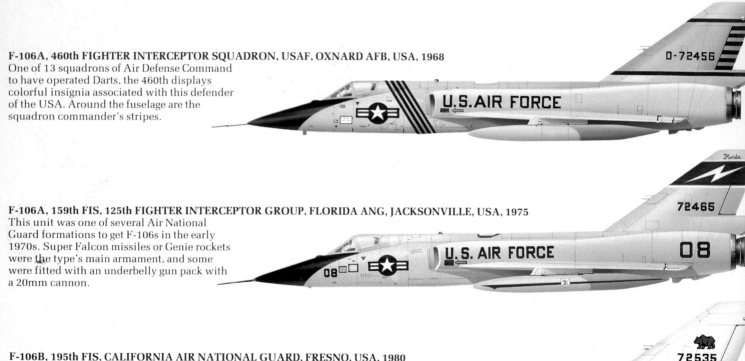

SAAB DRAKEN

Fighter interceptor; double delta wing design is still unique among the world's combat jets; still in service with Scandinavian air forces 35 years after the first prototype flew; nine attachment points for bombs, rockets or missiles.

J 35F, FLYGFLOTTILJ 10, SWEDISH AIR FORCE, ÄNGELHOLM, SWEDEN, 1970

For exercise purposes, a yellow checkerboard pattern has been applied over the camouflage of two greens on the fin. The design was repeated on the outer mainwheel doors and on the wing upper surfaces immediately inboard of the outer panels.

A 35XD (ALIAS F-35), ESK 725, ROYAL DANISH AIR FORCE, KARUP, DENMARK, 1977

A freshly painted aircraft in the matt finish prior to application of the gloss covering. Of 51 F 35, RF-35, and TF-35 Drakens originally bought by Denmark, eight are known to have been lost in accidents. An update program will keep the survivors flying for some years to come.

35XS, 11 SQUADRON, FINNISH AIR FORCE, ROVANIEMI, FINLAND, 1974

An unpainted aircraft assembled by Valmet in Finland from parts supplied by Saab. One of 12 in service, it later received a coat of camouflage paint and now operates alongside 11 others of its mark in a fleet of some 45 Drakens, both single and two-seaters.

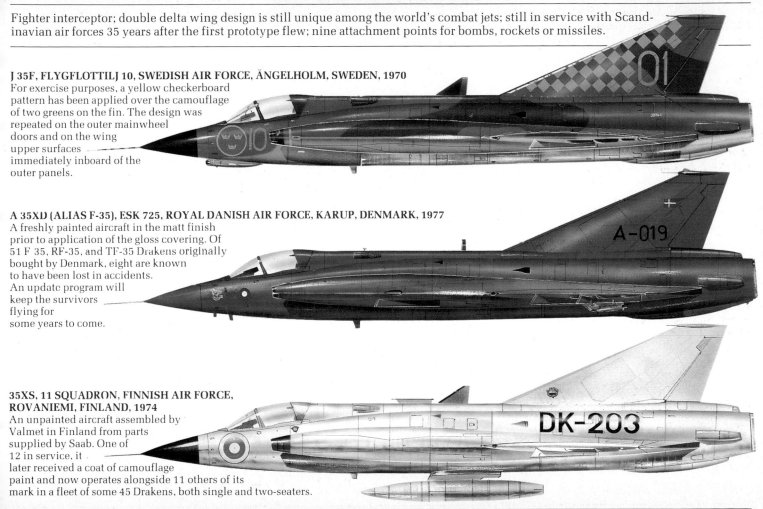

WESTLAND SEA KING

Anti-submarine warfare and transport; Westland-built version of the Sikorsky SH-3 Sea King; since first flight in 1969 there have been 14 versions; in service with the armed forces of Britain, West Germany, Australia, Belgium, Egypt, Norway, and Pakistan.

HC. Mk 4, 846 SQUADRON, RNAS YEOVILTON, UK, 1982
The finish of matt Olive Drab was applied to Commando assault versions during the Falklands conflict. The markings are toned down except for the tail rotor warning.

HAR, Mk 3, 22 SQUADRON, RAF, PORT STANLEY, FALKLANDS ISLANDS, 1982
An example of the Falklands conflict camouflage is shown here. Matt Dark Sea Gray has been applied over a Yellow search and rescue finish.

DASSAULT MIRAGE III

Fighter/interceptor and ground attack; was the first European fighter to attain Mach 2 in level flight (in 1958); versatility of the design has enabled production of trainer, recce and ground attack versions as well as a variant, the 5-series; production exceeds 1400.

IIIE, ESCADRON DE CHASSE 2/4 "LA FAYETTE," ARMEE-DE-L'AIR, LUXEUIL, FRANCE, 1977
Developed from the IIIC interceptor, the E version is a ground-attack aircraft with increased fuel and radar for blind, low-level navigation. This camouflage pattern was applied to a number of export aircraft. Note the indian head badge of the unit, which dates back to World War I.

IIIO, 77 SQUADRON, ROYAL AUSTRALIAN AIR FORCE, WILLIAMTOWN, AUSTRALIA, 1988
Australia operated Mirages from 1964 to 1988, and 100 single-seaters were delivered. One of the last schemes was this light gray finish; the "grumpy monkey" unit badge is on the fin. The Mirage has been replaced by the F-18 Hornet.

IIIEA, 1 ESCUADRON, VIII BRIGADA AEREA, ARGENTINE AIR FORCE, RIO GALLEGOS, ARGENTINA, 1982
During the Falklands conflict, Argentina's Mirage interceptors maintained air patrols to combat a possible RAF Vulcan strike against continental bases. The external load for these missions consisted of a Matra 530 and two Magic AAMs under fuselage and wings plus two 374 Imp gal drop-tanks

BRITISH AEROSPACE SEA HARRIER

Carrier-borne V/STOL fighter; operated by the Royal Navy and the Indian Navy; entered service with Royal Navy in 1980; unlike the Harrier has Blue Fox radar; during Falklands war Sea Harriers destroyed at least 20 Argentine aircraft without loss to themselves

FRS. Mk 1 800 SQUADRON, RNAS YEOVILTON, UK, 1981
This aircraft wears the pre-Falklands color scheme of semi-gloss Dark Sea Gray and Gloss White undersides. There is a Type D roundel in the wing and fuselage positions. The serial is almost invisible in the standard position below the tail plane.

FRS. Mk 1, 899 SQUADRON, ROYAL NAVY, HMS "HERMES," 1982
Painted Extra Dark Sea Gray overall for the South Atlantic campaigns. Note the Medium Sea Gray rear canopy framing.

Standard armament 'fit' for the air-to-air role, comprising Sidewinder missiles outboard, drop tanks and 30mm Aden gun pods under the fuselage.

BRITISH AEROSPACE HARRIER

V/STOL fighter/fighter-bomber; single Rolls-Royce Pegasus engine; revolutionized air-warfare as can operate without long runways; entered service in 1969; latest is GR.5/AV-8B operated by RAF and USMC; including Sea Harriers, 700 produced.

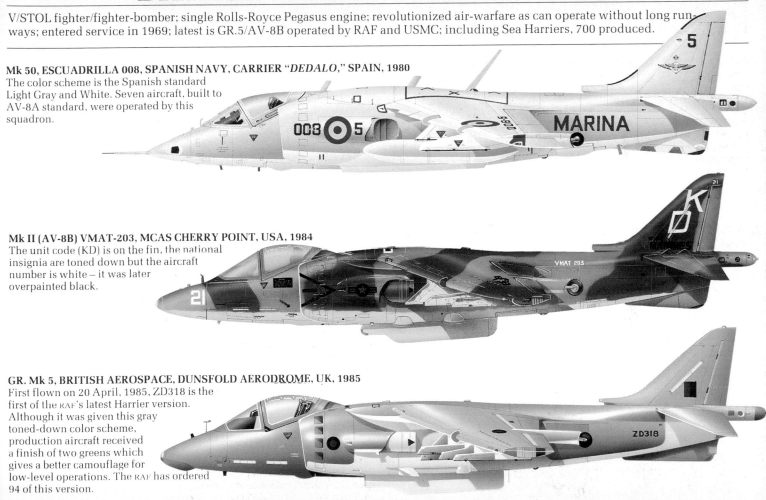

Mk 50, ESCUADRILLA 008, SPANISH NAVY, CARRIER "DEDALO," SPAIN, 1980
The color scheme is the Spanish standard Light Gray and White. Seven aircraft, built to AV-8A standard, were operated by this squadron.

Mk II (AV-8B) VMAT-203, MCAS CHERRY POINT, USA, 1984
The unit code (KD) is on the fin, the national insignia are toned down but the aircraft number is white – it was later overpainted black.

GR. Mk 5, BRITISH AEROSPACE, DUNSFOLD AERODROME, UK, 1985
First flown on 20 April, 1985, ZD318 is the first of the RAF's latest Harrier version. Although it was given this gray toned-down color scheme, production aircraft received a finish of two greens which gives a better camouflage for low-level operations. The RAF has ordered 94 of this version.

LOCKHEED P-3 ORION

Maritime patrol/anti-submarine warfare; development of the Lockheed Electra airliner; turboprop powered, the prototype first flew in August 1958; production P-3As entered service in 1962 and 641 were produced of all types.

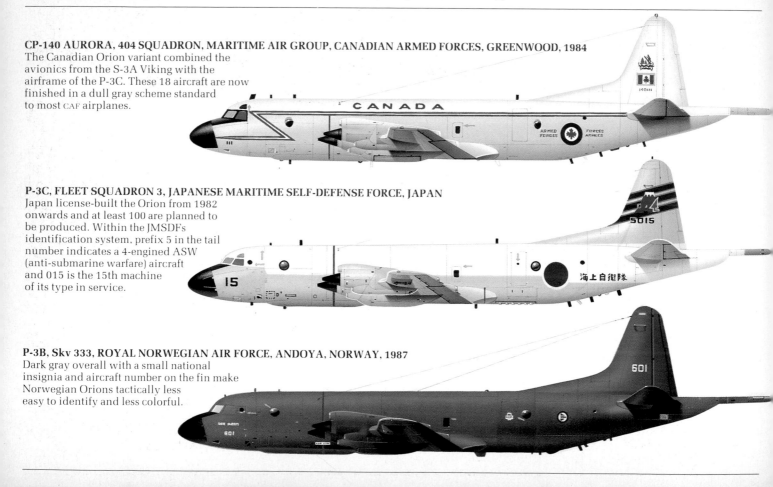

CP-140 AURORA, 404 SQUADRON, MARITIME AIR GROUP, CANADIAN ARMED FORCES, GREENWOOD, 1984
The Canadian Orion variant combined the avionics from the S-3A Viking with the airframe of the P-3C. These 18 aircraft are now finished in a dull gray scheme standard to most CAF airplanes.

P-3C, FLEET SQUADRON 3, JAPANESE MARITIME SELF-DEFENSE FORCE, JAPAN
Japan license-built the Orion from 1982 onwards and at least 100 are planned to be produced. Within the JMSDFs identification system, prefix 5 in the tail number indicates a 4-engined ASW (anti-submarine warfare) aircraft and 015 is the 15th machine of its type in service.

P-3B, Skv 333, ROYAL NORWEGIAN AIR FORCE, ANDOYA, NORWAY, 1987
Dark gray overall with a small national insignia and aircraft number on the fin make Norwegian Orions tactically less easy to identify and less colorful.

Fighter interceptor; initially designed for carrier-based operations with the US Navy, it was subsequently adopted by both the US MC and USAF; prototype F4H-1 first flew in 1958; in 1981, the 5201st and last new-build Phantom was produced.

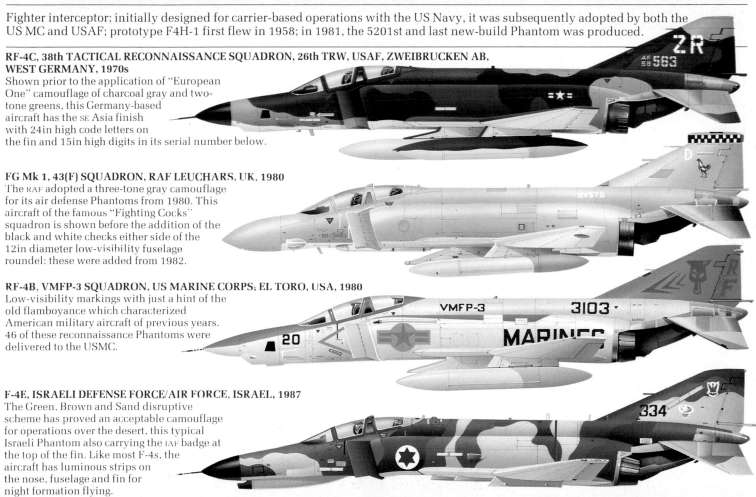

RF-4C, 38th TACTICAL RECONNAISSANCE SQUADRON, 26th TRW, USAF, ZWEIBRUCKEN AB, WEST GERMANY, 1970s
Shown prior to the application of "European One" camouflage of charcoal gray and two-tone greens, this Germany-based aircraft has the SE Asia finish with 24in high code letters on the fin and 15in high digits in its serial number below.

FG Mk 1, 43(F) SQUADRON, RAF LEUCHARS, UK, 1980
The RAF adopted a three-tone gray camouflage for its air defense Phantoms from 1980. This aircraft of the famous "Fighting Cocks" squadron is shown before the addition of the black and white checks either side of the 12in diameter low-visibility fuselage roundel: these were added from 1982.

RF-4B, VMFP-3 SQUADRON, US MARINE CORPS; EL TORO, USA, 1980
Low-visibility markings with just a hint of the old flamboyance which characterized American military aircraft of previous years. 46 of these reconnaissance Phantoms were delivered to the USMC.

F-4E, ISRAELI DEFENSE FORCE/AIR FORCE, ISRAEL, 1987
The Green, Brown and Sand disruptive scheme has proved an acceptable camouflage for operations over the desert, this typical Israeli Phantom also carrying the IAF badge at the top of the fin. Like most F-4s, the aircraft has luminous strips on the nose, fuselage and fin for night formation flying.

AEROSPATIALE ALOUETTE/III

Search and rescue/liaison; this aircraft was to establish Aerospatiale as Europe's leading helicopter company; of the 1455 machines produced, over 75 countries worldwide took delivery; it continues to appear in much modified form from other countries.

CHETAK, INDIAN AIR FORCE, 1984
The IAF operates both French-built and Hindustan Aeronautics-built Alouettes with an estimated 175 in service. Duties include SAR, liaison, training, etc.

SA 316B, 7 SQUADRON, ROYAL JORDANIAN AIR FORCE, AMMAN, JORDAN, 1981
Before their withdrawal from use, 16 machines were operated by the RJAF, including this example, numbered 318, which had a special communications 'fit' on board. The national roundel incorporates the seven-pointed star representing the first seven verses of the Koran.

BLACKBURN BUCCANEER

Maritime strike and ground attack aircraft; one of the world's finest low-level attack aircraft; prototype flew in 1958 and first production models went into service with the Royal Navy; transferred to RAF in 1979, some saw service in the Gulf War.

S Mk 2, 801 NAVAL AIR SQUADRON, HMS *VICTORIOUS*, ROYAL NAVY, 1965
Gloss-finished in Extra Dark Sea Gray and White, RN-operated aircraft were fitted with a "rhino horn" refueling probe to extend their range. Weapons were carried in the ventral rotating bomb bay.

S Mk 2, 809 NAVAL AIR SQUADRON, RNAS LOSSIEMOUTH, UK, 1969
A change in coloring for Buccaneers, to render them less visible in their low-level role, produced this overall gloss Extra Dark Sea Gray finish. On the fin is the unit badge, repeated in heraldic form on the engine intake.

S Mk 2B, 16 SQUADRON, RAF LAARBRUCH, WEST GERMANY, 1974
Replacing Canberras in the strike role as part of RAF Germany, Buccaneers were given a scheme of matt Dark Green, Dark Sea Gray and Light Aircraft Gray, then the RAF's standard disruptive finish. A bulged bomb bay fuel tank was fitted to increase the range; the nose probe was removed.

S Mk 50, 24 SQUADRON, SOUTH AFRICAN AIR FORCE, WATERKLOOF, SA, 1981
Only six aircraft of 16 ordered continue in SAAF use. A miniaturized national insignia has replaced the larger type originally applied. Gloss colors are Dark Sea Gray and PRU Blue undersides.

NORTHROP F-5

Fighter; designed as a low-cost, supersonic fighter; carried about 485 gallons of fuel, two 20mm cannon and two Sidewinder missiles; prototype first flew in July 1959 and entered production in 1962; over next 20 years some 30 countries acquired this small combat aircraft.

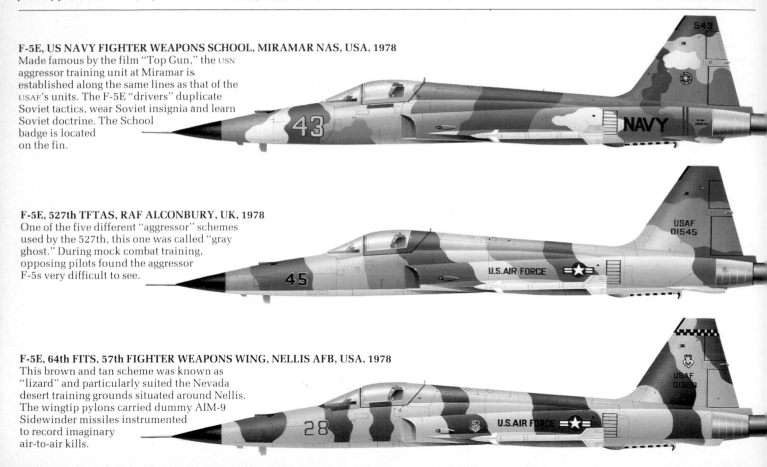

F-5E, US NAVY FIGHTER WEAPONS SCHOOL, MIRAMAR NAS, USA, 1978
Made famous by the film "Top Gun," the USN aggressor training unit at Miramar is established along the same lines as that of the USAF's units. The F-5E "drivers" duplicate Soviet tactics, wear Soviet insignia and learn Soviet doctrine. The School badge is located on the fin.

F-5E, 527th TFTAS, RAF ALCONBURY, UK, 1978
One of the five different "aggressor" schemes used by the 527th, this one was called "gray ghost." During mock combat training, opposing pilots found the aggressor F-5s very difficult to see.

F-5E, 64th FITS, 57th FIGHTER WEAPONS WING, NELLIS AFB, USA, 1978
This brown and tan scheme was known as "lizard" and particularly suited the Nevada desert training grounds situated around Nellis. The wingtip pylons carried dummy AIM-9 Sidewinder missiles instrumented to record imaginary air-to-air kills.

CF-5A/D, 434 "BLUENOSE" SQUADRON, CANADIAN ARMED FORCES, CHATHAM CFB, CANADA, 1980
Canadair-built CF-5As have a speed and climb rate superior to the basic F-5A. This example has the standard bi-lingual titling either side of the national marking on the nose and prominent squadron insignia on the fin and engine intakes. The refueling probe is an optional fitting and is used for long-range deployments.

RF-5E TIGEREYE, 17 SQUADRON, ROYAL SAUDI AIR FORCE, TABUK, SAUDI ARABIA, 1988
Tactical reconnaissance is the main task of the ten specialized Tigereye versions in Saudi service. Disruptive desert camouflage colors appear to be standard on RSAF Tornados, F-5s, Strikemasters and Hawks.

F-5E, 2nd FIGHTER WING, REPUBLIC OF CHINA AIR FORCE, TAIWAN, 1978
Another variation on the American SE Asia three-color camouflage which has been adopted by a number of air arms. This particular aircraft (74-00959) called 'Chung Chang' was one of an initial batch supplied by Northrop; subsequent machines were assembled at Taichung.

BELL IROQUOIS

Transport and fire-support; better known as the 'Huey', the UH-1 was the US forces workhorse in Vietnam; used for fire-support, cas-evac, logistical transportation, more than 20,000 were produced and they will still be around well into the 21st century.

UH-1B, 121st ASSAULT HELICOPTER CO, 13th COMBAT AVN BATTALION, US ARMY, SOC TRANG, VIETNAM, 1967
"BLITZ-KRIEG" of the "Vikings" armed (gunship) platoon. The national insignia had been removed from US Army UH-1s by this time, leaving them dark and dull apart from crew embellishments or the tactical marks as shown on this example.

UH-1B, 2/20th ARA, 1st CAVALRY DIVISION, US ARMY, VIETNAM, 1967
Armed with a Nord SS11 (US M22) anti-tank missile and carrying the famous Air Cavalry badge on the tail, this is a B Battalion machine. Inboard of the missiles is an XM-3 24 or 36-tube rocket-launcher pack.

UH-1D, 82nd MEDICAL DETACHMENT, 121st ASSAULT HELICOPTER CO, US ARMY, SOC TRANG, VIETNAM, 1967
Clearly marked with the time-honored red cross marking, this was a special medevac machine with space for six stretchers in the cabin. When the newer "Deltas" and "Hotel" versions first arrived in Vietnam they were assigned to the medevac units.

NORTH AMERICAN A-5

Carrier-based bomber and reconnaissance; problem concerning the linear bomb-bay effected its potential as a bomber, instead 59 early models were converted to RA-5C multi-sensor recce aircraft and gave valuable service in Vietnam; total production 156.

A3J-1 (A-5A), VAH-7, US NAVY, USS *ENTERPRISE*, AUGUST 1962
The first full squadron deployment at sea saw this early version aboard *Enterprise*. The bomber had a noticeably flat-topped fuselage compared with the humped appearance of the later RA-5C. Colors were Light Gull Gray and Gloss White, with the unit badge on the side of the engine intake.

RA-5C, RVAH-6 "FLEURS," US NAVY, USS *CONSTELLATION*, LATE 1960s
Built as an A-5A bomber this machine was assigned to the Pacific Fleet, as indicated by the NL tail code. Under the fuselage is a side-looking radar pod which also contained cameras. The nose number denotes the squadron and aircraft number (4) within the squadron.

RA-5C, RVAH-13, US NAVY, USS *INDEPENDENCE*, SE ASIA, EARLY 1970s
For over-land recce operations, a coat of standard SE Asia camouflage was deemed advisable, and late in the Vietnam conflict, aircraft like this became a familiar sight on Yankee Station in the Gulf.

GRUMMAN A-6 INTRUDER

Bomber; all-weather attack aircraft with crew of two; can deliver 18,000lbs of bombs over a 1,000 mile range, a feat regularly demonstrated in Vietnam; many flown by the US Navy from carriers and heavily involved in Gulf War operations.

A-6E, VA-65 "TIGERS," US NAVY, USS *INDEPENDENCE* (CVW-7), 1974

Shown before the addition of the chin-mounted sensor turret known as TRAM (Target Recognition And Multi-sensor), which is on most E versions, this example is in the standard scheme of non-specular Light Gull Gray with Glossy White undersides. Bright unit markings were still part of the operational scene.

EA-6A, VMCJ-2, US MARINES, DA NANG, VIETNAM, 1972

Replacing the EF-10B Skyknight, this Intruder version provided tactical ECM for Marine strike operations in SE Asia. Unlike other A-6s, the EA-6A had no wingtip speed brakes, relying instead on one on each side of the rear fuselage for aerodynamic braking (seen here under the word "MARINES").

A-6E, VA-128, US NAVY, NAS WHIDBEY ISLAND, USA, MID-1980s

The low-visibility finish had really taken effect by this time and units were allowed to display their markings only in outline form, usually on the tail. This squadron was the Pacific Fleet replacement training unit. The grays used are 36320 (dark) on the upper surface and 36375 (light) on the undersides.

EA-6B, VAQ-134, US NAVY, USS *ENTERPRISE* (CVW-14), LATE 1970s

In the lengthened fuselage the Prowler carries a four-man crew which includes two ECM operators in the rear seats. Located under the wings and belly are powerful jamming pods. The unusual "rhino-horn" in front of the cockpit is the aerial refueling probe.

SEPECAT JAGUAR

Ground attack/maritime strike; jointly developed by BAC and Dassault-Breguet; single-seat all-weather attack version and two-seat trainers produced; Britain and France ordered some 200 each and a number sold overseas to India, Ecuador, Nigeria, and Oman.

GR Mk 1, 14 SQUADRON, RAF BRÜGGEN, WEST GERMANY, 1984
The RAF received 202 Jaguars, almost all camouflaged in Dark Green and Dark Sea Gray. Low visibility national markings were somewhat compromised by the brightness of the squadron badge, but this would have been toned down or removed in wartime. Under the wing is a 264 Imp gal drop-tank.

JAGUAR A, EC 1/7 "PROVENCE," FRENCH AIR FORCE, ST DIZIER, FRANCE, 1983
Armée de l'Air purchased 160 single-seat As and 40 two-seat Es to equip nine Escadrons in 3, 7 and 11 Escadres de Chasse. Aircraft deployed overseas to Africa had their European camouflage oversprayed in a sand and stone coloring.

JAGUAR INTERNATIONAL, 8 SQUADRON, SULTAN OF OMAN'S AIR FORCE, THRUMRAYT, OMAN, 1981
Dark Earth and Light Stone applied over all surfaces is the scheme adopted for the low-level attack role in this barren country. In recent years the small tail insignia has been changed, with blue replacing the red.

M-B-B BO105

Communications/anti-tank; as BO105M used for liaison and communications by West German Army; later BO105P with uprated transmission and improved rotors was selected for anti-tank use; armed with six HOT or eight TOW anti-tank missiles.

BO105P, WEST GERMAN ARMY AVIATION, 1985

Three *Panzerabwehrregiments* home-based at Celle, Roth and Fritzlar are equipped with the anti-tank version of the BO105. Each of the 212 machines can carry six HOT wire-guided missiles, the gunner using a roof-mounted sight to acquire the targets.

BO105GSH, BATTALION DE HELICOPTEROS DE ATAQUE I, SPANISH ARMY AVIATION, SPAIN, 1986

Assembled in Spain by CASA, the BO105 operates with the Army in three main roles, anti-tank (Spanish designation HA.15), reconnaissance (HR.15) and attack with a 20mm cannon installation under the fuselage (also HR.15).

VOUGHT A-7 CORSAIR

Carrier-based fighter/bomber; smaller than the F-8 Crusader, A-7As were delivered to the US Navy in 1966; the A-7E continues to serve with the US Navy powered by a license-built Rolls-Royce Spey turbofan; production of all marks totaled 1545.

A-7E, VA-25 "FISTS OF THE FLEET," LIGHT ATTACK WING PACIFIC, USN, NAS LEEMORE, USA, 1975
Shown when operating from the carrier USS *Ranger* (CV-61) this Corsair is finished in the then-standard Light Gull Gray and Gloss White scheme. The Squadron is now designated VFA-25 and operates the F-18 Hornet.

A-7E, VA-27 "ROYAL MACES," LIGHT ATTACK WING PACIFIC, USN, NAS LEEMORE, CALIF
This unusual camouflage was one of several experimental low-visibility schemes tried in the mid-Seventies and comprised blue, light blue and tan uppersurfaces with light blue undersides. White was deleted from the insignia. The unit was operating from the USS *Enterprise* (CVN-65) at the time.

A-7D, 23rd TACTICAL FIGHTER WING, USAF, ENGLAND AFB, LATE 1970s
"Wraparound" camouflage came into effect on USAF Corsairs in the late 1970s. In October 1977, this unit won every award in a Tactical Bombing Competition against the Royal Air Force at RAF Lossiemouth, Scotland. The 23rd subsequently converted to the A-10A Thunderbolt.

SIKORSKY CH-53/S-65

Rescue and recovery helicopter/mine-countermeasures; with the Chinook, the largest Western helicopter in service, it joined the Marines in 1966, successful in Vietnam, the CH-53 was also involved in the abortive 1980 Iranian hostage rescue mission.

HH-53C, 37th ARRS, US AIR FORCE, DA NANG AB, SOUTH VIETNAM, 1971

The premier rescue helicopter in SE Asia, Super Jolly Green Giants roamed across the jungles of North and South Vietnam.

The long nose refueling probe for air-to-air refueling allowed extended missions to be flown in search of downed aircrew. Miniguns were often the only defensive armament for these large machines.

CH-53D, HMH-462, US MARINE CORPS, FUTENMA, OKINAWA, LATE 1970s

Dark olive drab made these helicopters often appear almost black in daylight. Apart from the rescue and warning markings, all other insignia was applied in black. Sea Stallion is the official name of Marine-operated CH-53A/Ds.

CH-53C, 601st TASS, USAF, SEMBACH AB, W GERMANY, EARLY 1980s

'European 1' camouflage pattern was sprayed on the small force of USAF CH-53C Super Jollies based in W Germany and New Mexico, USA. Official Tech Order color names are Gunship Greens 34092 and 34102 and Gunship Gray 36118, the numbers relating to the Federal Standard 595a list.

RH-53D, HM-12, US NAVY, NAS NORFOLK, USA, 1975
The tremendous power of the H-53 prompted
the USN to order a minesweeping version, the
RH-53A. The later D variant, of
which 30 were built,
succeeded it and HM-12 was the first
Helicopter Mine Countermeasures
Squadron. The structure under the
rear fuselage is used to tow the
mine sweep gear.

MH-53H, 1st SPECIAL OPERATIONS WING, USAF, HURLBURT FIELD, USA, 1987
Night and adverse weather operations called
for this modification of the HH-53C.
Equipment includes Forward-
Looking Infra-Red,
Doppler navigation system and, in the nose
thimble, radar taken from the A-7D
Corsair II.

CH-53E, HC-1, US NAVY, NORTH ISLAND, CALIF, 1985
USN Super Stallions adopted this very dark
gray finish principally for night
operations although
it is also effective coloring against
the sea. All markings appear
pale blue with just the
machine number (441) in
white. The external
fuel tanks on the E
version
each carry
650 US gal.

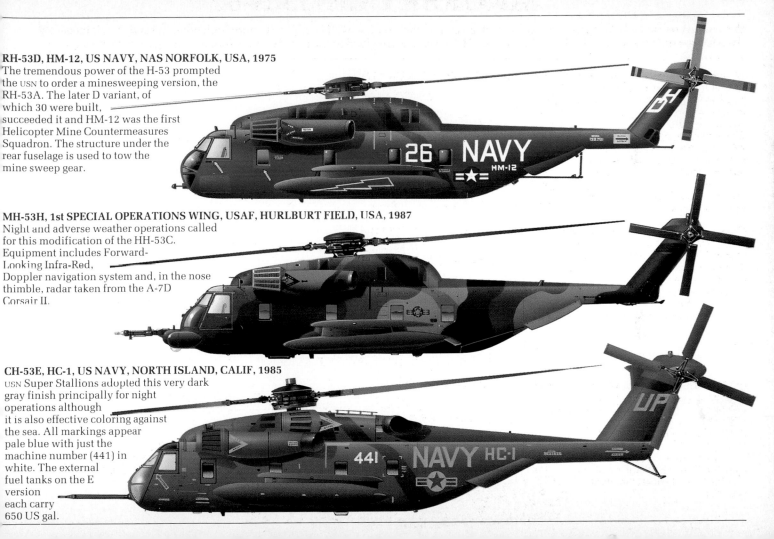

LOCKHEED F-104

Fighter interceptor; the single-seat Mach 2 Starfighter was dubbed, 'the missile with a man in it!' when it first appeared; it entered USAF service in 1958 and was manufactured under license in Europe and Japan, with a total of 2406 built.

F-104G, 30th TACTICAL FIGHTER WING, REPUBLIC OF CHINA AIR FORCE, CHING CHUAN KANG, TAIWAN, 1987
This Vietnam-style SE Asia camouflage is just one of a number of finishes to be seen on Taiwan-based combat aircraft. More than 100 F-104s have been acquired by the RCAF from other air forces to supplement their F-5Es.

F-104S, FILO, 9 AIR BASE, TURKISH AIR FORCE, BALIKESHIR, TURKEY, 1987
This disruptive camouflage scheme was applied to all 40 new-built F-104S aircraft bought from Italy in the Seventies. Just about half remain flyable alongside some older F-104Gs.

TF-104G, JABOG 32, WEST GERMAN AIR FORCE, LECHFELD, WEST GERMANY, 1967
The coding system of two letters and three digits divided by the cross was discontinued by the Luftwaffe in 1968 and replaced by four numbers. Under the early system, DB related specifically to Jabog 32.

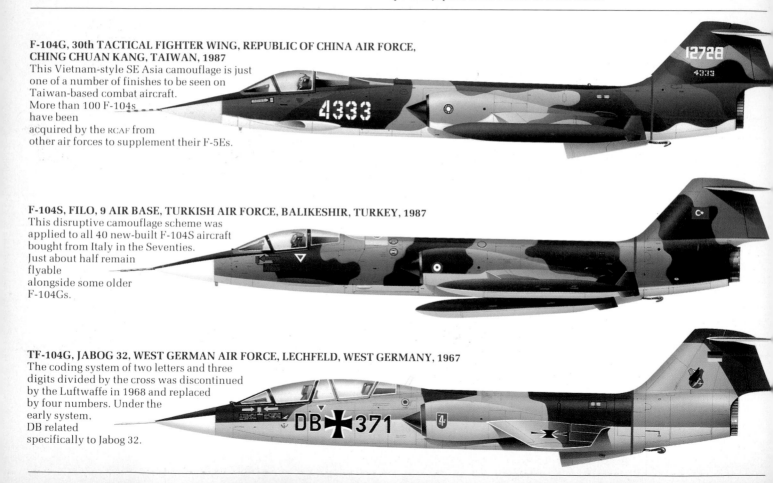

BRITISH AEROSPACE STRIKEMASTER

Light trainer and ground attack; two-seater powered by a Rolls-Royce Viper engine; developed from the Jet Provost basic trainer, its functional design proved particularly robust on ground-attack duties in the Middle-East's harsh climate.

Mk 87, KENYA AIR FORCE, KENYA, 1971
Six were delivered in 1971 with Dark Green, Dark Sea Gray and Light Aircraft Gray undersides. Five were still in use in 1988.

Mk 80, ROYAL SAUDI AIR FORCE, RIYADH, SAUDI ARABIA, 1973
The white on green flag inscription on the fin reads "There is no God but Allah, and Muhammad is the Prophet of Allah." Unit codes are in both Arabic and Roman numerals.

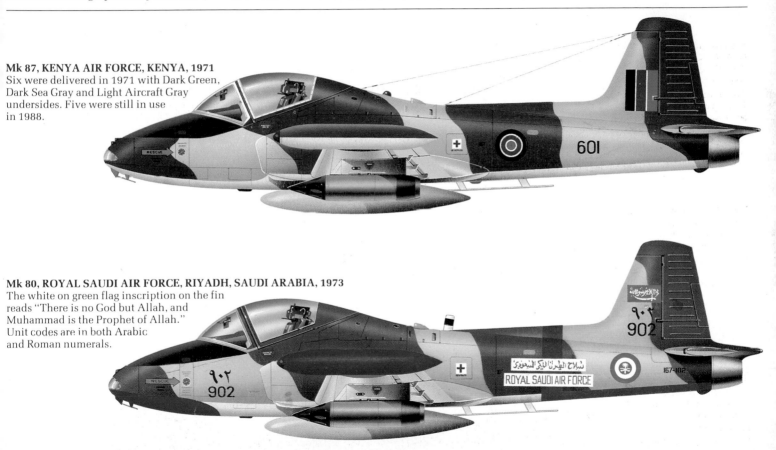

GENERAL DYNAMICS F-111

All-weather bomber; capable of delivering laser-guided bombs thousands of miles from its base, the F-111 underwent a stormy development; the F-111B was ordered by the US Navy as a carrier-based aircraft but then canceled; production reached 562.

F-111F, 493rd TACTICAL FIGHTER SQUADRON, 48th TFW, USAF, LAKENHEATH, UK, 1983

The ultimate model, with more powerful engines than previous versions and more advanced avionics. In the April 1986 attack on Libya, 13 F-111Fs took part, some using 2000lb laser-guided bombs carried underwing, as shown in this view. One aircraft was lost on the operation, code-named "El Dorado Canyon."

F-111C, 1 and 6 SQUADRONS, ROYAL AUSTRALIAN AIR FORCE, AMBERLEY, AUSTRALIA, 1984

A8-146 is one of 24 C versions purchased by the RAAF. It combines the basic F-111A airframe, engines and avionics with the long-span wings of the FB-111A bomber. This example has SE Asia camouflage with miniaturized insignia and unit lightning flash on the fin.

EF-111A, 366th TACTICAL FIGHTER WING, USAF, MOUNTAIN HOME AFB, USA, 1982

Grumman converted 42 F-111As into the defense and electronic-warfare EF-111A nicknamed "Electric Fox" and officially called Raven. Finished in the two-tone gray scheme, a number of aircraft are also based in the UK to support European F-111A operations. Note the TAC badge on the rudder and unit badge by the cockpit.

Light armed reconnaissance; the 'Bronco' won a joint USAF/Navy/Marine Corps competition for a Light Armed Reconnaissance Aircraft and could carry two crew and five paratroops as well as a range of equipment and weapons; production totaled 390.

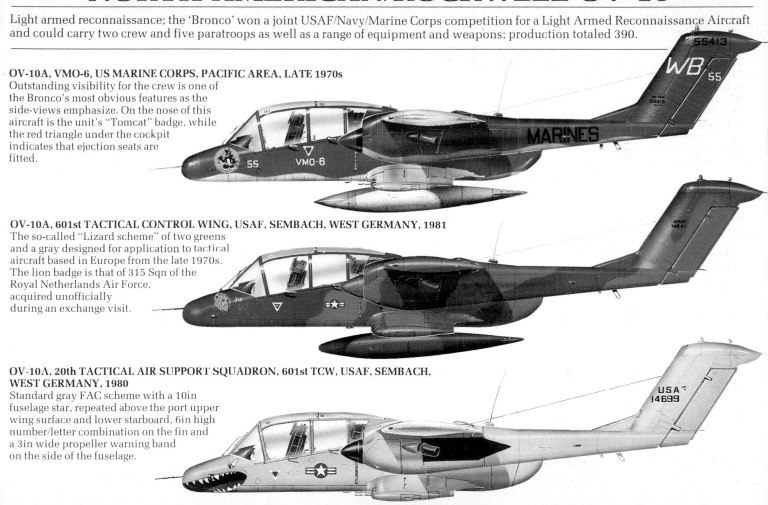

OV-10A, VMO-6, US MARINE CORPS, PACIFIC AREA, LATE 1970s
Outstanding visibility for the crew is one of the Bronco's most obvious features as the side-views emphasize. On the nose of this aircraft is the unit's "Tomcat" badge, while the red triangle under the cockpit indicates that ejection seats are fitted.

OV-10A, 601st TACTICAL CONTROL WING, USAF, SEMBACH, WEST GERMANY, 1981
The so-called "Lizard scheme" of two greens and a gray designed for application to tactical aircraft based in Europe from the late 1970s. The lion badge is that of 315 Sqn of the Royal Netherlands Air Force, acquired unofficially during an exchange visit.

OV-10A, 20th TACTICAL AIR SUPPORT SQUADRON, 601st TCW, USAF, SEMBACH, WEST GERMANY, 1980
Standard gray FAC scheme with a 10in fuselage star, repeated above the port upper wing surface and lower starboard, 6in high number/letter combination on the fin and a 3in wide propeller warning band on the side of the fuselage.

BEECH KING AIR

Liaison, communications and trainer; the American Beech-built King Air succeeded the Queen Air of the 1960s and an updated, larger Super King Air followed, which could seat 14 in its pressurized cabin.

T-44A, TAW-4 UNITED STATES NAVY, NAS CORPUS CHRISTI, USA, 1977

The US Navy bought more than 60 of these executive "twins" for multi-engine training replacing old, expensive piston-engined aircraft. The gloss red and white scheme is a safety measure, but also provides an attractive finish.

C-12A, US AIR FORCE, ISLAMABAD, PAKISTAN, 1986

A total of 30 of these Super King Air Model 200s were bought for attaché and military assistance advisory missions throughout the world. Other variants in use include the C-12F, the C-12J version of the Beech 1900 airliner and the US Army's C-12A Huron.

RC-12D, MILITARY INT. BATTALION, US ARMY, SOUTH KOREA, 1987

Code-named *Guardrail V* and used for battlefield reconnaissance, this electronic warfare-configured "twin" is a good example of how changed some previously-inocuous looking executive can become. All but anonymous, the aircraft is finished in medium gray.

Fighter/fighter bomber; various versions known as the 'Flogger' series; the MiG Bureau delivered the variable geometry MiG-23 to the Soviet Air Force in the early 1970s; the MiG-27, was called the 'Flogger D' and there have been many types in service.

MiG-23 "FLOGGER G," SOVIET AIR FORCE, KUBINKA AB, MOSCOW, 1978
Green, brown and tan best sums up the tactical camouflage on this machine. The ventral fin on the Flogger series folds through 90° for landing and take-off.

MiG-27 "FLOGGER D," SOVIET FORCES, EAST GERMANY, 1978
Compared with the fighter versions, this attack aircraft has a sharply tapering nose to give the pilot better visibility. On the wing pylon of this aircraft is a multiple ejector rack for bombs, and there are other weapon pylons under the fuselage and on each side behind the wing.

MiG-23BM "FLOGGER F," CZECHOSLOVAK AIR FORCE, PARDUBICE, CZECHOSLOVAKIA, 1980
This is the attack version of the interceptor, designed for export customers. It retains the basic airframe but incorporates a new chisel nose for the attack role (note the intake and exhaust areas and compare them with the Soviet Flogger D above).

FOKKER F27

Transport or marine patrol; the turbine-engined Friendship has been sold to 63 countries and 25 air arms; the Dutch AF version is known as 'Troopship,' while 'Maritime' is the designation of Fokker's over-water patrol variant.

Mk 300M TROOPSHIP, 334 SQUADRON, ROYAL NETHERLANDS AIR FORCE, SOESTERBERG, NETHERLANDS, 1975

Twelve aircraft were delivered to the RNAF in 1960–1, including three Mk 100s, each initially capable of troop and cargo use. Some were later converted to other roles, including C-5 which was camouflaged in green and gray in 1971 and changed to become a navigation trainer.

Mk 400M, TRANSPORT SQUADRON, FINNISH AIR FORCE, UTTI, FINLAND, 1985

This is one of three aircraft used for most of the logistic tasks with the air arm. In addition to the freight door forward, large rear doors permit paradrops from both sides of the aircraft. The other two machines are coded FF-1 and FF-2.

Mk 400, SÉNÉGAMBIA AIR FORCE, DAKAR, SÉNÉGAMBIA, 1986

Six F27s were bought in the late 1970s for transport duties when the air arm was the Sénégalese Air Force. Sénégal has since merged with The Gambia to form one country. Like a number of military transport fleets, this one has civil registrations applied to its aircraft.

AEROSPATIALE/WESTLAND PUMA

Transport helicopter; prototype flew in 1965, being designed to meet French Air Force requirements; versions of the type, including the improved performance Super Puma, have been ordered by 25 armed forces and can seat up to 16 troops.

HC Mk 1, 230 SQUADRON, RAF GÜTERSLOH, WEST GERMANY, 1982
Special events call for special markings. In this case, the tiger motif in its badge qualified the squadron for attendance at the 1982 Tiger Meet, calling for a color scheme with a difference. A good effect by the ground crew – who had to return the aircraft to its standard scheme after the event.

AS.332L, EJERCITO DE CHILE, TOBALADA, CHILE, 1986
Main identifying features of the Super Puma are the additional fin under the tail, larger main wheel sponsons and a more pointed nose. This is one of three purchased in 1983, of which two survive.

BOEING CH-47 CHINOOK

Medium transport helicopter; the US Army required the twin-rotor Chinook in Vietnam for its battlefield mobility and few were lost; two versions are in production, the CH-47D, and derivatives like the special forces version, the MH-47E; it has sold worldwide.

CH-47C, UNITED STATES, ARMY, TAN SON NHUT, VIETNAM, 1972

Dubbed "The Hook" (and less printable nicknames) by the GIs in SE Asia, the Chinook provided the important heavy airlift required by the war in the South. Olive Drab overall was standard, as was the forward hatch-mounted MG.

HC Mk 1, 18 SQUADRON, RAF, PORT SAN CARLOS, FALKLAND ISLANDS, JUNE 1982

"Bravo November" was the sole survivor of the Exocet attack on the *Atlantic Conveyor* container ship on 25 May 1982. Camouflaged in Dark Green and Dark Sea Gray, this machine flew almost continuously until the Argentine surrender some three weeks later. The call-sign letter BN appeared on the front and rear rotor pylon in black.

CH-47C, ROYAL MOROCCAN AIR FORCE, RABAT, MOROCCO, 1988

A desert sand and stone camouflage was applied to the 12 Italian-built Chinooks delivered for logistic support along the country's borders. Note the five-letter code above the tail emblem.

Single-seat fighter or two-seat trainer; the Su-7's greatest asset is its rugged simplicity because the 'Fitter' lacked both the range and weapon load to be a successful warplane; Sukhoi later designed more efficient swing-wing aircraft – the Su-17, -20 and -22 series.

Su-7BMK, V-VS (SOVIET AIR FORCE), TRANS-BAIKAL MILITARY DISTRICT, USSR, 1978
Wearing a tactical camouflage of dark green, earth, and light blue, this Soviet-operated "Fitter A" carries two 600-liter drop-tanks on the fuselage pylons and UV-16-57 rocket pods under the wings.

Su-7UM, EGYPTIAN AIR FORCE, CAIRO WEST AIRFIELD, EGYPT, 1976
To give conversion training on the type, the two-seat -7UM was produced. The instructor in the rear seat uses a periscope to see ahead, but his view remains limited. "Moujik" (peasant) is the West's name for the trainer version.

Su-7BM, ALGERIAN AIR FORCE, 1977
Another of the Soviet Union's Middle Eastern export clients. Algeria received about 20 of the "Fitter A" version. The pod at the base of the rudder is the tail parachute housing; by the wing-root gun is a steel anti-blast panel to protect the fuselage skin.

GRUMMAN F-14 TOMCAT

Carrier-based fighter; the latest addition to Grumman's 'cat' family, the F-14 entered service in 1972 and over 600 have been delivered; regular improvements have been effected to the engines (from TF30s to F110 turbofans), radar, avionics, and armament.

F-14A, VF-32 US NAVY, USS *JOHN F. KENNEDY*, MID-1970s

Combat proven and victor in a few short, sharp exchanges with Libyan Soviet-made MiG-23 Floggers and Su-22 Fitters, the F-14 is heavily advantaged with its long-range radar and associated Phoenix missiles. Every safety-conscious, the Navy insisted on a whole range of stencil instructions to be applied to the airframe, an example of which is visible on the nose.

F-14A, VF-1 "WOLFPACK," US NAVY, NELLIS AFB, USA, 1977

Aviation artist Keith Ferris devised this experimental finish, designed to break up the outline of the F-14. Three shades of gray in hard-edged splinter style were used, and in some cases no markings were applied. Several aircraft took part in the trials, others coming from VF-2 and VX-4. The schemes have not been adopted to date.

F-14A, VF-103 "SLUGGERS," US NAVY, USS *SARATOGA*, 1983

Gray outline markings, subdued unit tail insignia, but a black 211 on the nose with the last two digits repeated at the tip of the fin for identification when parked on deck. The number is also repeated on the flaps, so that "flyco" on the island can identify the aircraft as it moves to the catapult for launching.

Anti-tank helicopter; the Mi-24 bore the brunt of hill fighting against the *Mujahideen* in Afghanistan; the Hind is armed with either 12.7mm MG in a chin turret or a twin barrel 30mm cannon on right-hand fuselage side, plus a range of ground-to-air ordnance.

Mi-24 (HIND D), SOVIET ARMEISKAYA AVIATSIYA, USSR, 1984
Factory-applied sand and stone camouflage appears as standard on most Soviet-operated Hinds, although green sometimes replaces the darker color. A tail-rotor warning is applied on the rear fuselage, and on the boom is the aircraft number in yellow.

Mi-24 (HIND D), AFGHAN REPUBLICAN AIR FORCE, KABUL, AFGHANISTAN, 1985
Hinds flew extensively as convoy escorts and also on search-and-destroy missions in the mountains. The advent of Stinger and Blowpipe SAMs forced crews to stay out of the missiles' range.

Mi-24 (HIND D), IRAQI AIR FORCE, BAGHDAD, IRAQ, 1985
For operations against Iranian forces this Iraqi Hind has been given an additional national flag marking on the forward fuselage, presumably to aid identification over the battlefield.

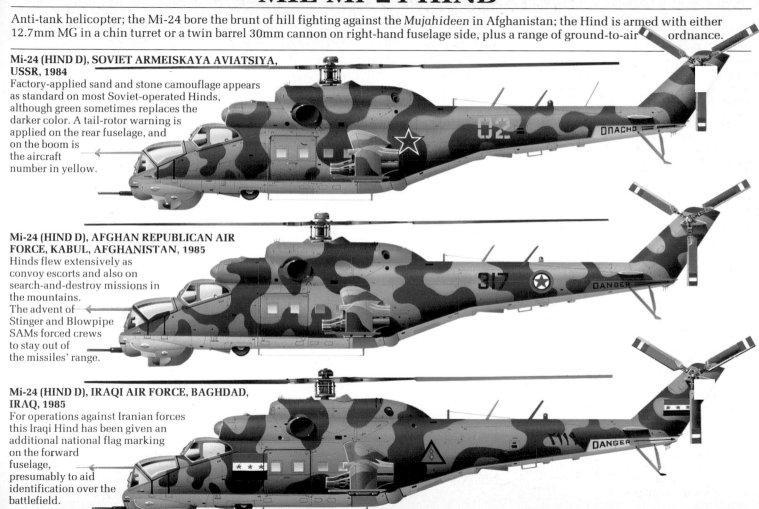

DASSAULT MIRAGE F.1

Interceptor-fighter-bomber; like its delta-winged Mirage III predecessor, Dassault's Mirage F.1 has enjoyed considerable export success, with many of the 730 manufactured going to ten international air arms as well as to the French Air Force.

F.1CE, ESCUADRON 141, ALA DE CAZA 14, SPANISH AIR FORCE, ALBACETE, SPAIN, 1980

May 1975 and 04 was one of the first batch of aircraft delivered to Spain, the second nation to order the interceptor. Internal armament of the F.1 consists of two 30mm cannon located under the intakes.

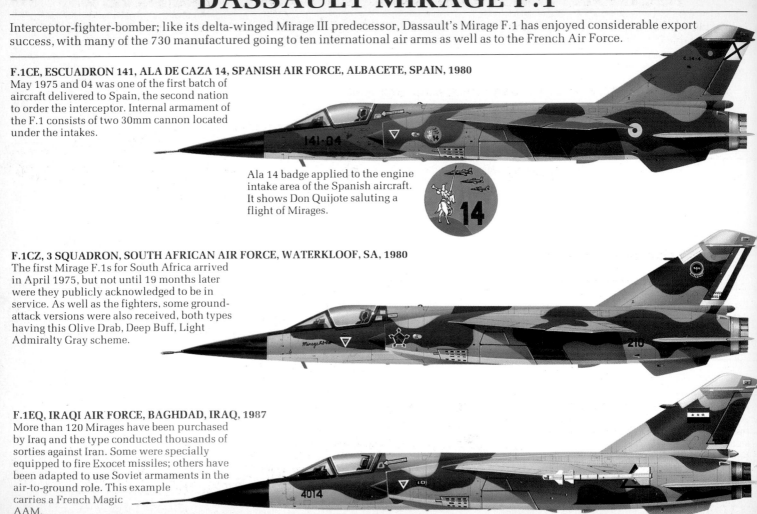

Ala 14 badge applied to the engine intake area of the Spanish aircraft. It shows Don Quijote saluting a flight of Mirages.

F.1CZ, 3 SQUADRON, SOUTH AFRICAN AIR FORCE, WATERKLOOF, SA, 1980

The first Mirage F.1s for South Africa arrived in April 1975, but not until 19 months later were they publicly acknowledged to be in service. As well as the fighters, some ground-attack versions were also received, both types having this Olive Drab, Deep Buff, Light Admiralty Gray scheme.

F.1EQ, IRAQI AIR FORCE, BAGHDAD, IRAQ, 1987

More than 120 Mirages have been purchased by Iraq and the type conducted thousands of sorties against Iran. Some were specially equipped to fire Exocet missiles; others have been adapted to use Soviet armaments in the air-to-ground role. This example carries a French Magic AAM.

Multi-role combat jet; the twin-engined Hornet was developed from the Northrop YF-17, flying in prototype form in November 1978; carrier-capable it entered the US Navy and Marine service in 1980, subsequently being ordered by Australia, Canada, and Spain.

F-18A, VFA-131, CARRIER AIR WING 7, USS *DWIGHT D. EISENHOWER*, 1990
The latest US Navy scheme on an F-18A of VFA-131 'Wildcats' in June 1990. The undersurface color (36495) has been replaced with an overall finish of Light Compass Ghost Gray used previously only on top.

F/A-18, US MARINE CORPS, EL TORO, CALIFORNIA, MID-1980s
Painted in the early 'low viz' scheme which dates the illustration to pre-1988. The lower surfaces are Gray (36495), the top surfaces Light Compass Ghost Gray and the anti-glare panel forward of the cockpit is Gray-Blue. VAMFA-531 is appropriately named 'Gray Ghosts.'

CF-18A, 409 TACTICAL FIGHTER SQUADRON, BADEN SOLLINGEN, GERMANY, 1990
Apart from the unusual full-color unit badge on the fins, this aircraft of the 'Nighthawk' squadron has the standard scheme of Gray-Blue (FS.595a: 35327) uppersurfaces, Light Compass Ghost Gray undersurfaces (36375) and a Sea Gray (36118) false canopy under the nose.

McDONNELL DOUGLAS F-15 EAGLE

Fighter; designed to replace the Phantom, the Eagle is the USAF's primary air superiority fighter; five versions have been produced: F-15A and C are single-seaters, B and D two-seaters, and E two-seat fighter and interdiction; 1266 manufactured in total.

F-15A, 5th FIGHTER INTERCEPTOR SQUADRON, USAF, MINOT AFB, USA, 1986
Third US air defense squadron to receive F-15s in June 1985, the 5th FIS applied this decorative finish over the Compass Gray scheme. On the fin is the TAC (Tactical Air Command) badge and behind the engine intake is the unit badge. The external fuel tank holds 600 US gal.

F-15E, McDONNELL DOUGLAS, ST LOUIS, MS, DECEMBER 1986
First prototype "Strike Eagle" in the markings applied for early trials. The first operational USAF unit is the 4th TFW at Seymour Johnson AFB, SC. USAF plans to procure a total of 392 F-15Es.

F-15A, 133 SQUADRON, ISRAEL DEFENSE FORCE/AIR FORCE, ISRAEL, 1977
One of the first F-15s to be delivered to the IDF/AF, this example carries Sparrow and Sidewinder missiles, both weapons used to some effect against Syrian MiGs.

LOCKHEED S-3 VIKING

Carrier-based submarine hunter; the standard fixed-wing aircraft with US Navy ASW squadrons; the has wings and fin which fold and a retractable MAD boom at the tail for carrier storage; in all, 187 'computer with wings' were made.

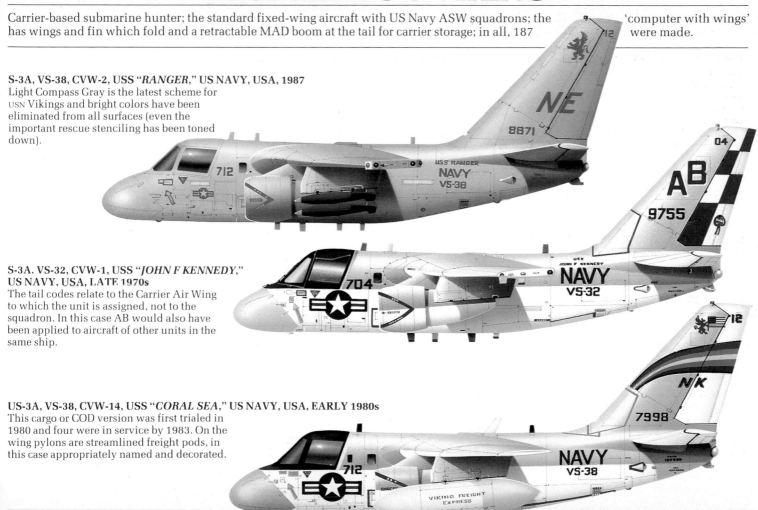

S-3A, VS-38, CVW-2, USS "RANGER," US NAVY, USA, 1987
Light Compass Gray is the latest scheme for USN Vikings and bright colors have been eliminated from all surfaces (even the important rescue stenciling has been toned down).

S-3A. VS-32, CVW-1, USS "JOHN F KENNEDY," US NAVY, USA, LATE 1970s
The tail codes relate to the Carrier Air Wing to which the unit is assigned, not to the squadron. In this case AB would also have been applied to aircraft of other units in the same ship.

US-3A, VS-38, CVW-14, USS "CORAL SEA," US NAVY, USA, EARLY 1980s
This cargo or COD version was first trialed in 1980 and four were in service by 1983. On the wing pylons are streamlined freight pods, in this case appropriately named and decorated.

BRITISH AEROSPACE HAWK

Advanced trainer and attack aircraft; the RAF introduced the Hawk to replace the Gnat and Hunter types, and ten air arms across four continents have ordered them; T-45 Goshawks, for the US Navy, and Hawk 200 single seaters have also been developed.

T Mk 1, NO 1 TACTICAL WEAPONS UNIT, RAF BRAWDY, UK, 1980

Bearing the "shadow squadron" insignia of 234 Sqn, this aircraft has the standard matt Dark Green and Dark Sea Gray camouflage for the low-level tactical training role. The serial number is repeated in white on the fin.

Crest of the Tactical Weapons Unit.

T Mk 1A, NO 2 TACTICAL WEAPONS UNIT, RAF CHIVENOR, UK, 1985

Satin-finish Medium Sea Gray with Barley Gray undersides is the low-visibility finish for this Sidewinder-armed aircraft. The insignia is pink and light blue. Note that Hawks wired to fire Sidewinder missiles are designated T Mk 1A.

T-45 GOSHAWK, US NAVY, 1987

Early impression of the Gloss White and Orange-colored future Navy trainer. The actual machine has undergone a number of changes to the airframe since this drawing, but the colors are believed to be substantially correct.

FAIRCHILD A-10

Ground attack; the A-10 'Warthog's' two engines are in an unusual position to reduce the effect of heat emissions at
missiles; the widely-spaced fins, and massive wings, which carry up to seven tons of ordnance, make the aircraft ea

YA-10, US AIR FORCE, EDWARDS AFB, USA, LATE 1976

The second prototype, with the port wing and
outside port fins painted white for photo-
graphic orientation in spinning tests.
On the nose is a test probe, and
the fin shape
is different from that
eventually adopted for
production aircraft.

A-10A, 354th TACTICAL FIGHTER WING, USAF, MYRTLE BEACH, USA, 1977

This was the scheme chosen after the
camouflage trials as standard for all
production aircraft from serial No 75–280
onwards. All markings were dulled
with black outline "star and
bar," badges, rescue and
maintenance stenciling
and the unit/base code
on the fin.

A-10A, 23rd TACTICAL FIGHTER WING, USAF, ENGLAND AFB, USA, 1983

When the light gray finish was found to be
too contrasting "down among the trees," the
so-called Lizard scheme was adopted and still
exists on A-10s. The shark-mouth
surrounds the 30mm seven-barreled
cannon, while on the fin tip is
the squadron color. Lizard
color reference to FS595a:
Green (34103), Green
(34092), Gray (36081).

SIKORSKY H-60

...1 support helicopter; orders for the combat survivable replacement for the Bell UH-1 Huey exceeding 2700 have been received
...2 countries (2253 for the US Army); the Black Hawk or naval-based Seahawk can carry 11 soldiers or an 8000lb under slung load.

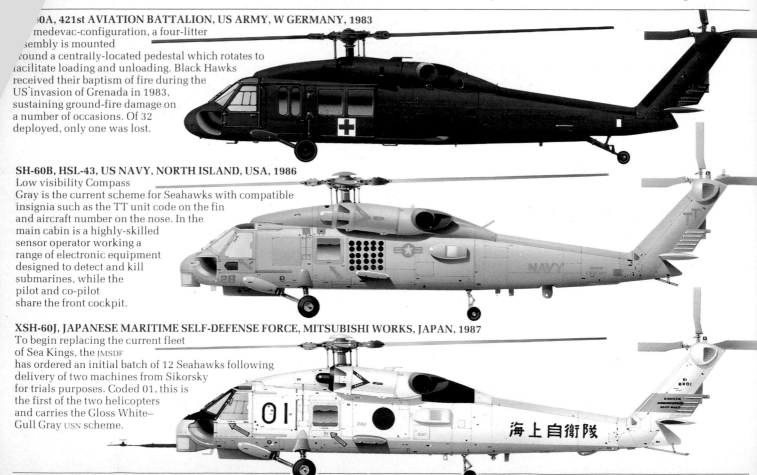

...60A, 421st AVIATION BATTALION, US ARMY, W GERMANY, 1983
...medevac-configuration, a four-litter
...sembly is mounted
...round a centrally-located pedestal which rotates to
facilitate loading and unloading. Black Hawks
received their baptism of fire during the
US invasion of Grenada in 1983,
sustaining ground-fire damage on
a number of occasions. Of 32
deployed, only one was lost.

SH-60B, HSL-43, US NAVY, NORTH ISLAND, USA, 1986
Low visibility Compass
Gray is the current scheme for Seahawks with compatible
insignia such as the TT unit code on the fin
and aircraft number on the nose. In the
main cabin is a highly-skilled
sensor operator working a
range of electronic equipment
designed to detect and kill
submarines, while the
pilot and co-pilot
share the front cockpit.

XSH-60J, JAPANESE MARITIME SELF-DEFENSE FORCE, MITSUBISHI WORKS, JAPAN, 1987
To begin replacing the current fleet
of Sea Kings, the JMSDF
has ordered an initial batch of 12 Seahawks following
delivery of two machines from Sikorsky
for trials purposes. Coded 01, this is
the first of the two helicopters
and carries the Gloss White–
Gull Gray USN scheme.

WESTLAND LYNX

Utility/ASW/anti-tank helicopter; has been at the forefront of design since its 1971 debut; equipped with TOW anti-armor missiles and Sea Skua at sea, they are used on anti-tank or anti-submarine duties; the 400 helicopters manufactured are operational all round the world.

HAS, Mk 3, 815 SQUADRON, RNAS PORTLAND, UK, 1988
The overall scheme of semi-gloss Dark Sea Gray has proved ideal for over-water flying. The letters "PO" are Portland base initials.

HAS. Mk 2 (FN) FLOTTILLE 31F, FRENCH AERONAVALE, LANVEOC-POULMIC, 1987
This example has an overall dark blue-gray finish, with the unit badge beneath the cockpit side window.

Mk 21, 1 ESQUADRAO DE HELICOPTEROS ANTI-SUBMARINOS, BRAZILIAN NAVY, SAO PAULO DE ALDEIA, 1987
Nine Lynx were bought by Brazil of which eight are in service. The finish is semi-matt.

GENERAL DYNAMICS F-16

Fighter; the F-16 will probably go down in history as the fighter of the 1980s; single and two-seat versions are both combat capable, and its distinctive, diminutive-tailed delta shape symbolizes western air defense; more than 3000 aircraft have been ordered by 16 air forces.

F-16A, 8th TACTICAL FIGHTER WING, USAF, KUNSAN AB, SOUTH KOREA, 1986

The C is steadily replacing the older A series aircraft and this unit has now re-equipped. By the cockpit is the "Wolfpack" marking next to the unit badge. National markings are toned down although the tail codes and serial remain black. Camouflage colours:
(dark) Gray (36118),
(medium) Gray (36270),
(light) Gray (36375).

Plan view of the top colour demarcation used by most F-16 operations.

F-16B, TACTICAL AIR COMMAND, USAF, HILL AFB, USA, 1980

Aircraft 79-0096 was used to evaluate the "Lizard" camouflage scheme of two greens and gray for possible use by F-16 units in Europe. To date this has not been adopted.

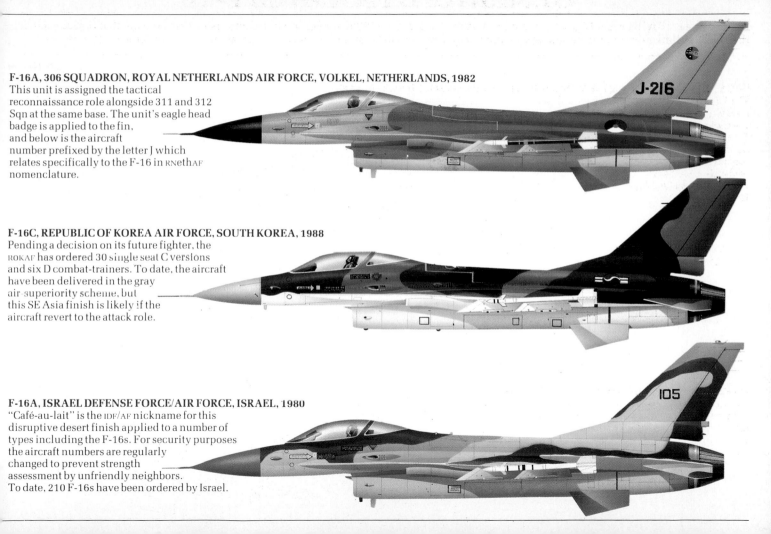

F-16A, 306 SQUADRON, ROYAL NETHERLANDS AIR FORCE, VOLKEL, NETHERLANDS, 1982
This unit is assigned the tactical reconnaissance role alongside 311 and 312 Sqn at the same base. The unit's eagle head badge is applied to the fin, and below is the aircraft number prefixed by the letter J which relates specifically to the F-16 in RNethAF nomenclature.

F-16C, REPUBLIC OF KOREA AIR FORCE, SOUTH KOREA, 1988
Pending a decision on its future fighter, the ROKAF has ordered 30 single seat C versions and six D combat-trainers. To date, the aircraft have been delivered in the gray air-superiority scheme, but this SE Asia finish is likely if the aircraft revert to the attack role.

F-16A, ISRAEL DEFENSE FORCE/AIR FORCE, ISRAEL, 1980
"Café-au-lait" is the IDF/AF nickname for this disruptive desert finish applied to a number of types including the F-16s. For security purposes the aircraft numbers are regularly changed to prevent strength assessment by unfriendly neighbors. To date, 210 F-16s have been ordered by Israel.

PANAVIA TORNADO

Fighter interceptor/fighter-bomber; one of the most successful international programs in aerospace history, it was developed by the UK, Germany, and Italy to meet a common requirement; total orders have reached 929 including Saudi Arabia and Oman.

GR Mk 1, 9 SQUADRON, RAF HONINGTON, UK, 1985
Previously flying Vulcans, this unit with its famous bat insignia was the first RAF squadron to convert to Tornados. The Dark Green/Dark Sea Gray camouflage wraps around the whole aircraft apart from the black nosecone. Total RAF GR Mk 1 orders in 1989 stood at 255.

TORNADO, 7 SQUADRON, ROYAL SAUDI AIR FORCE, DHAHRAN, SAUDI ARABIA, 1986
Sand, stone and green are the camouflage colors of the first 48 aircraft on order for this Arab air arm. All machines carry the squadron number as a prefix to the tail number. The wing insignia is applied to the port upper and starboard lower positions, with the initials RSAF in the opposing positions.

F Mk 2, 229 OCU, RAF CONINGSBY, UK, 1986
One of the initial 18 fighter versions which preceded the definitive F Mk 3. Armament of the air defense variant consists of Skyflash and Sidewinder AAMs and an internal 27mm cannon. The pale Barley Gray finish is standard on all operational machines. The F.2s will be updated to F.3 standard and will be redesignated F.2As.

MIKOYAN-GUREVICH MiG-29 FULCRUM

Fighter; Russia's current front-line tactical supersonic fighter, it was designed by the Mikoyan bureau; armed with a 30mm cannon and a range of air-to-air guided missiles carried underwing, the 'Fulcrum' is capable of Mach 2 and has a look down/shoot down radar.

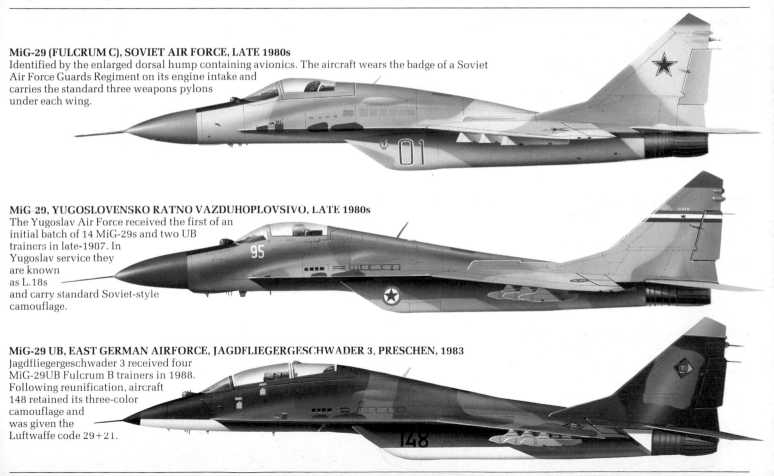

MiG-29 (FULCRUM C), SOVIET AIR FORCE, LATE 1980s
Identified by the enlarged dorsal hump containing avionics. The aircraft wears the badge of a Soviet Air Force Guards Regiment on its engine intake and carries the standard three weapons pylons under each wing.

MiG-29, YUGOSLOVENSKO RATNO VAZDUHOPLOVSIVO, LATE 1980s
The Yugoslav Air Force received the first of an initial batch of 14 MiG-29s and two UB trainers in late-1907. In Yugoslav service they are known as L.18s and carry standard Soviet-style camouflage.

MiG-29 UB, EAST GERMAN AIRFORCE, JAGDFLIEGERGESCHWADER 3, PRESCHEN, 1983
Jagdfliegergeschwader 3 received four MiG-29UB Fulcrum B trainers in 1988. Following reunification, aircraft 148 retained its three-color camouflage and was given the Luftwaffe code 29+21.

INDEX